AF167753

Transformational Tools for Special Educators

This book is dedicated to the extraordinary professionals in special education whose commitment, resilience, and heart transform lives in countless ways.

And to my husband, Charles, whose steadfast support sustained me through every chapter of this work.

Transformational Tools for Special Educators

How to Beat Burnout and Become the Best at What You Do

Katrina G. Huels

CORWIN

FOR INFORMATION:

Corwin

A Sage Company

2455 Teller Road

Thousand Oaks, California 91320

(800) 233-9936

www.corwin.com

Sage Publications Ltd.

1 Oliver's Yard

55 City Road

London EC1Y 1SP

United Kingdom

Sage Publications India Pvt. Ltd.

10th Floor, Emaar Capital Tower 2

MG Road, Sikanderpur

Sector 26, Gurugram

Haryana - 122002

India

Sage Publications Asia-Pacific Pte. Ltd.

18 Cross Street #10-10/11/12

China Square Central

Singapore 048423

Copyright © 2026 by Corwin Press, Inc.

All rights reserved. Except as permitted by U.S. copyright law, no part of this work may be reproduced or distributed in any form or by any means, or stored in a database or retrieval system, without permission in writing from the publisher.

When forms and sample documents appearing in this work are intended for reproduction, they will be marked as such. Reproduction of their use is authorized for educational use by educators, local school sites, and/or noncommercial or nonprofit entities that have purchased the book.

All third-party trademarks referenced or depicted herein are included solely for the purpose of illustration and are the property of their respective owners. Reference to these trademarks in no way indicates any relationship with, or endorsement by, the trademark owner.

No AI training. Without in any way limiting the author's and publisher's exclusive rights under copyright, any use of this publication to "train" generative artificial intelligence (AI) or for other AI uses is expressly prohibited. The publisher reserves all rights to license uses of this publication for generative AI training or other AI uses.

A Cataloging-in-Publication number is available from the Library of Congress.

ISBN: 979-8-3488-3497-5

Vice President and
   Editorial Director: Monica Eckman

Senior Acquisitions Editor: Jessica Allan

Associate Editor: Melissa Rostek

Production
   Editor: Veronica Stapleton Hooper

Copy Editor: Lynne Curry

Typesetter: C&M Digitals (P) Ltd.

Graphic Designer: Gail Buschman

DISCLAIMER: This book may direct you to access third-party content via web links, QR codes, or other scannable technologies, which are provided for your reference by the author(s). Corwin makes no guarantee that such third-party content will be available for your use and encourages you to review the terms and conditions of such third-party content. Corwin takes no responsibility and assumes no liability for your use of any third-party content, nor does Corwin approve, sponsor, endorse, verify, or certify such third-party content.

Contents

Foreword

Steve McMahon

Over thirty years ago, I walked into my first special education classroom with a teaching degree, good intentions, and no understanding of what I was about to face. I had no idea I was entering a profession that would demand every ounce of my emotional intelligence, resilience, and capacity for human connection.

This book is a timely and essential resource for a profession in crisis. Special education teachers are among the most highly stressed professionals in our society, and burnout isn't just a buzzword. It is a devastating reality driving talented educators out of the field at alarming rates. The problem isn't a lack of dedication from our teachers. It's that we've failed to equip them with the emotional intelligence skills essential for thriving in these high-stress, high-stakes environments.

Over the years, I've worn many hats: special education teacher, program specialist, behavior intervention consultant, and now CEO of MindSet Safety Management. Each role has deepened my understanding of a fundamental truth: The most critical skills we need in special education aren't found in any teaching manual. They're the skills of emotional regulation, crisis de-escalation, and maintaining our humanity under extreme pressure.

As a teacher, I learned that student behavior is communication—but I wasn't prepared for how that communication would trigger my own stress responses. Moving into program specialist and behavior intervention roles, I began to see patterns: The most effective educators weren't necessarily those with the most training: They were those who could stay calm in chaos, read the emotional climate of a room, and respond thoughtfully rather than reactively.

This is where Katrina Huels's work becomes invaluable. With a strong background in psychology and over twenty-two years of experience in special education, Katrina has identified the missing piece in professional development for special educators. The tools she presents in this book represent exactly what we've needed: evidence-based strategies for developing the emotional infrastructure that makes excellence sustainable in our field. More importantly, these are the critical skills necessary for personal wellness that will improve overall school culture and teacher retention.

Special education is a series of cascading challenges requiring real-time decision-making under emotional stress. What makes this book different from typical wellness advice is that it doesn't offer platitudes about self-care or generic stress management tips. Instead, it treats emotional intelligence as professional development—sophisticated skills that can be learned, practiced, and mastered. The neuroplasticity research underlying these tools means that with practice, staying calm under pressure can become as automatic as any other professional skill.

What I appreciate most about this approach is its foundation in a growth model. Just as we wouldn't expect a student to master reading without consistent practice, we can't expect ourselves to develop emotional intelligence skills without deliberate, ongoing application. This book doesn't offer quick fixes or one-size-fits-all solutions. Instead, it provides a systematic framework for building competencies that grow stronger with repetition.

The beauty of this growth model is that it mirrors what we know works with our students. We start with basic skills, practice them until they become automatic, then build upon that foundation. Each chapter provides not just the theory but also the practical techniques that must be rehearsed, refined, and integrated into daily practice. Whether it's learning to use breathwork in the moment of crisis or developing empathy through perspective-taking exercises, these skills become more natural and effective the more we use them.

This practice-based approach acknowledges that emotional intelligence isn't something we either have or don't have. It is a set of learnable skills that improve with intentional effort. The real-world scenarios and step-by-step techniques provide the structured practice opportunities we need to develop these capacities. These tools can be applied throughout all roles in our society, but they're especially crucial for those of us working on the front lines of education.

To every educator, administrator, paraprofessional, and support staff working in schools today: You are on the front lines of one of society's most important missions. The work you do matters, and you deserve tools that match the significance of your calling.

This book should be in the hands of every person working in education—not as another requirement to add to your workload but as the professional development you've been waiting for. The emotional intelligence skills Katrina presents here aren't just beneficial; they're essential for creating the kind of educational environment where both staff and students can thrive. In a profession where burnout threatens our most dedicated professionals, this book offers a path toward sustainable excellence built on skill rather than willpower alone.

Steve McMahon

CEO, MindSet Safety Management and
author of *Transformative Crisis Management*

Publisher's Acknowledgments

Corwin gratefully acknowledges the contributions of the following reviewers:

Rachel Avlia
Special Education Consultant
Heartland AEA
Johnston, IA

Jennifer Crotts
Assistant Principal/Teacher
Gwinnett County Public Schools
Lawrenceville, GA

Dr. Rebecca Dennis-Canges
Professor
Metropolitan State University of Denver
Denver, CO

Teri Fechter
Special Education Teacher
Appleton Area School District
Appleton, WI

Louis Lim
Principal
Bur Oak Secondary School
Markham, Ontario, Canada

Debra Paradowski
Associate Principal; NASSP Assistant Principal of the Year (2020)
Mukwonago High School
Mukwonago, WI

Erin Schons
Assistant Director of Schools
Children's Home Society
Sioux Falls, SD

Janet Wyatt-Ross
Assistant Principal
Fayette County Public Schools
Lexington, KY

About the Author

 **Katrina G. Huels** is an educational consultant who has more than twenty years of experience in special education, with expertise spanning instructional design, program leadership, and national accreditation. She has served in roles ranging from classroom teacher to senior executive, and her robust background in psychology and education informs a career grounded in evidence-based practice and systemic reform. Throughout her career, Katrina experienced firsthand both the profound rewards and the ongoing stress and fatigue that lead to burnout among educators. As she sought strategies to build internal balance, resilience, and motivation in herself and her staff members, she encountered a persistent gap in resources and a lack of systemic solutions.

Drawing on the framework of emotional intelligence and the science of neuroplasticity, Katrina translates research into actionable tools tailored to high-stakes environments. This work reflects her conviction that all educators deserve strategies that allow them to thrive in their roles throughout their careers. You can find more information and contact Katrina at https://www.huelsappliedharmony.com.

Introduction

I have been privileged to work alongside special educators in a variety of roles, from classroom teacher to executive leadership. Most of us enter special education from a place of purpose, driven by a belief in every student's potential and a desire to make a positive difference. But the daily realities of the work can take a toll in unexpected ways.

When special educators lose passion for their work or leave the field entirely, it is rarely because they stopped caring about students. The problem is that so few are equipped with the tools needed to care for themselves in the same way they care for others. Without clear strategies to navigate the ongoing stress and demands inherent to the field, professionals often find themselves counting down the days until the next calendar break, wondering how much longer they can endure the strain.

Throughout each school year, special educators receive extensive training on legal compliance, specialized instruction, and behavior management. Yet, where is the professional learning that supports the professionals? When considering your own experience, how many training sessions have addressed stress reduction and burnout prevention? Very few options like this exist, and when they do appear, they rarely meet the emotional and cognitive demands of the special educator's role. This gap in professional development is not just unfortunate. It is unsustainable, and it feeds directly into the burnout crisis that is pushing special educators out of the field. This is not just a systemic problem. It is deeply personal.

THE CHALLENGE

The challenges in special education are formidable, regardless of your role. It may be the mounting paperwork and extensive data collection, the behavioral crises, the complex IEP meetings that become adversarial, the budget constraints that leave programs under-resourced, or the constant juggling of multiple priorities and stakeholder needs. Whether you are managing a caseload, leading a team, overseeing compliance, or supporting families through difficult decisions, the relentless demands can feel overwhelming.

You are not alone. Nearly half of all K-12 teachers report feeling burned out often or always, with special educators facing particularly high rates of stress and turnover. Simply enduring the strain and hoping for relief is not a solution. There is an urgent need to develop the emotional and psychological skills currently omitted from our professional preparation. Special education professionals require resources and professional development that move beyond best practices and creative classroom interventions. They need practical tools to create internal and external environments where they can excel and thrive throughout their careers.

THE SOLUTION

Transformational Tools for Special Educators is a practical, research-informed toolkit designed to help special education professionals mitigate stress, without adding to an already overwhelming workload.

The tools in this book are not theoretical concepts or generic wellness advice. Research-based tools are presented here within the context of each emotional intelligence domain (self-awareness, self-regulation, motivation, empathy, social skills) and paired with real-world scenarios in special education settings. This approach provides a deep understanding of the tools in contexts that reflect your daily experience. The content emphasizes underlying neurological mechanisms and the research behind each tool, so that you understand *how* the tools work and *why* they work. You will gain perspective on why consistent application reshapes the brain in ways that support you regardless of the challenges you encounter. This work is not about managing stress in the moment. It is about training your nervous system to respond differently over time.

THE IMPACT

As you strengthen your emotional intelligence, you become a steadying force in your school community. Your regulated nervous system helps co-regulate others. Your students feel safer and more supported. Your colleagues experience you as a reliable source of guidance and professionalism. Families trust you more readily. The ripple effects of your neurological transformation create positive change throughout your entire professional ecosystem.

When districts integrate this work into professional development curricula, they can expect greater staff retention, more responsive leadership, productive teams, improved student outcomes, and a supportive school culture that fosters long-term engagement and satisfaction.

WHO WILL BENEFIT FROM THIS WORK

Whether you are a first-year teacher feeling overwhelmed by the complexity of your role, a veteran educator experiencing chronic fatigue, a related service provider or social worker juggling multiple schools, or an administrator seeking to support your team more effectively, this resource meets you where you are. The content here is particularly relevant for special education teachers, paraeducators, and a wide range of specialists, including social workers, speech-language pathologists, occupational therapists, adaptive coaches, and behavior specialists. School and district administrators will also find valuable tools and insights to support themselves and their teams here.

HOW TO APPROACH THIS WORK

Transformational Tools is designed to be used individually or at the school, district, or state levels.

If used individually, you can read the book in its entirety, or you can choose to focus on the areas where you need the most support right now, whether that's staying calm under pressure, maintaining motivation when progress feels slow, or building stronger relationships with the families and colleagues you serve. There is no need to master everything at once. Just start using the tools and trust in your brain's remarkable capacity for change, and when you do, you will realize that most of the tools provided here can be implemented in just three to ten minutes and integrate seamlessly into your existing routines.

If implemented at the school or district level through professional learning, a training curriculum and consultative support are available, or you can use the book on its own to guide professional development or professional learning community studies.

Chapter 3 provides a full guide to the book's structure and suggestions for how to begin. You will also find a breakdown of how each tool is presented, including practical techniques, real-world scenarios, and key neurological insights to support long-term application.

Whether you start at the beginning or jump to a section aligned with your current challenges, the tools are flexible enough to support you now and in the future.

The remarkable individuals who serve exceptional students deserve a practical, science-backed guide that offers lasting support throughout their professional journey. This book delivers that resource.

PART 1

Setting the Stage:
The Crisis, the Science, and the Framework

CHAPTER 1

The Burnout Crisis

I used to wake up excited to make a difference. Now, I wake up exhausted, wondering how much longer I can do this.

J. Tobert, Special Education Supervisor

Chronic fatigue, one of the many precursors to burnout, lies at the root of Mr. Tobert's sentiments. His thoughts and feelings are shared by educators nationwide, and this type of exhaustion undermines motivation and erodes the hope of sustaining a fulfilling career in special education.

Burnout is a state of chronic physical, emotional, and mental exhaustion that results from prolonged exposure to unrelenting stress.[1] In special education, it often emerges when professionals are expected to meet multiple demands without the resources, support, or time to do so effectively. Burnout is cumulative, often beginning with subtle signs like emotional depletion or a sense of detachment. If left unaddressed, this can lead to a profound loss of motivation, diminished professional efficacy, and a sense of disconnection from one's work and purpose. When burnout takes hold, it affects a person's cognition, mood, and even physical health.

Special education professionals understand the profound impact of their work. Most would agree that the rewards of the profession are vast and undeniable, but so are the challenges. Balancing diverse student needs with mounting responsibilities and limited resources is taking a toll.

It is important to understand that the impact of burnout is not confined to the individual experiencing it, especially in the workplace. When a person begins to struggle with feelings of overwhelm and fatigue, performance naturally declines. Emails may go unanswered. Collaboration with colleagues becomes inconsistent. Communication with families is delayed or reduced. Sick days increase. Paperwork piles up. Gradually, essential responsibilities fall behind, and the burden shifts to others. This redistribution of tasks creates a cascading effect that adds pressure to colleagues who already manage full workloads. When half of a special education team shows signs of burnout, the entire system risks destabilization, and the ability to function as a coordinated team breaks down.

These patterns are not isolated or rare. They appear in schools and districts across the country, pointing to an issue that is reshaping the profession itself. Burnout is widespread, measurable, and accelerating. To find effective solutions, understanding the full scope and impact of the burnout crisis is essential.

SCOPE AND IMPACT

Burnout among educators is reaching critical levels. Chronic stress, emotional depletion, and unsustainable workloads are pushing professionals to their limits. Psychologist Herbert Freudenberger first defined burnout in 1974 as emotional exhaustion in caregiving professions,[2] and it remains one of the greatest challenges in education.

Recent statistics further underscore the scope of the problem:

- In 2024, nearly 44 percent of K–12 teachers in the United States reported feeling burned out often or always.[3]

- Gallup research identified K–12 teachers as the most burned-out professionals, with 52 percent reporting extreme stress, higher than in any other profession.[4]

- Educators early in their careers are particularly vulnerable; up to 50 percent leave the field within their first five years.[5]

The crisis is even more pronounced for special education teachers. Special education teacher turnover stands at 15 percent annually, with numbers continuing to rise.[6] In Pennsylvania, for example, special education departures increased from 17 percent in 2019–2020 to 22 percent in 2021–2022.[7] By the 2023–2024 school year, more than half of US school districts and 80 percent of states reported shortages of special education teachers.[8]

These statistics are not surprising and reflect daily realities. A special education teacher might spend the morning differentiating lessons for students with complex learning profiles, then shift to crisis intervention for a student in emotional distress, and finally attend a lengthy Individualized Education Program (IEP) meeting that includes family members, administrators, and attorneys. The relentless pace of these responsibilities, often performed with limited breaks or resources, gradually erodes balance and well-being.

Though the burnout crisis in special education is often associated with teachers, it impacts the entire network of professionals supporting students with special needs, as noted in Table 1.1.

TABLE 1.1 Burnout Factors for Special Education Professionals

PROFESSION TITLES	BURNOUT FACTORS
Speech-language pathologists	Typically manage caseloads of 50 to 60 students across multiple schools. They must balance a wide range of responsibilities, including direct therapy, paperwork compliance, and collaboration with educators and families. Working in multiple locations can sometimes lead to professional isolation and logistical challenges that further increase stress.[9]
Occupational therapists	Juggle a myriad of tasks, from designing and implementing individualized interventions, developing IEP goals, to collaborating with teachers and families. A survey of school-based occupational therapists in Colorado found that although most occupational therapists spend their workweek on direct services, a substantial portion of their time is tied up in evaluative, consultative, and documentation-related tasks, suggesting that rising demands reduce time available for direct therapy.[10] The increasing complexity and demands for school-based practitioners increase the risk for burnout.[11]
Paraeducators	Provide valuable classroom and one-on-one support for students who have significant behavioral or medical needs, often without adequate recognition, wages, or support.[12] There is limited research specific to rates of burnout for paraeducators, but the demands of this role coupled with feeling unappreciated and underpaid easily sets the stage for stress and fatigue that leads to burnout.
School counselors	Play a critical role in student well-being. The American School Counselor Association (ASCA) recommends a ratio of one counselor per 250 students, but in reality, the national average is closer to one per 380 students, with some states exceeding 1 to 600.[13]
School social workers	Coordinate services for students experiencing poverty, homelessness, or significant mental health challenges. Their work involves not only supporting students but also advocating for families. Research highlights that school workers are experiencing burnout linked to unrealistic workloads, role conflict, and a lack of resources.[14]
Behavior analysts	Support students with significant behavioral concerns throughout their workday, often without adequate staffing support. A study found that over 70 percent of Board Certified Behavior Analysts reported experiencing burnout, with emotional exhaustion and depersonalization being the most commonly cited factors.[15]
School and district leaders	Navigate an educational landscape that includes staff shortages, compliance mandates, and increasing student needs. Many spend their days resolving crises, managing personnel, and shouldering the emotional weight of supporting both students and staff. A 2021 article report shared research findings found that 42 percent of school administrators had considered resigning because of working conditions, high-stakes accountability, lack of decision-making authority, and a lack of professional learning opportunities. stress, workload, and lack of support.[16]

Across the country, schools are losing qualified special education profession-als faster than they can replace them.[17] Burnout contributes heavily to special education positions that remain vacant for months.[18] When left unaddressed, service delivery weakens, support teams fragment, and a cycle of staff turn-over leaves students without the consistency they need.[19] The more burnout spreads, the more it reshapes the profession by attrition.

Burnout is not only drawing experienced special educators out of the field, it actively discourages others from entering it. College students preparing to enter the special education field are expressing growing concern about the stress, isolation, and unrealistic demands reported by current educators.[20]

While some level of stress is inherent to special education, especially as the number of students requiring intensive support continues to rise,[21] burnout is not an unavoidable outcome. What can change is how schools structure their systems, how leaders prioritize staff well-being, and how individual professionals approach their own sustainability in the field. Research-based methods and tools are available that can turn the tide on the burnout trend.

A PATH FORWARD

The challenges in special education are significant, but they do not have to define the profession. With the right tools and resources, professionals who serve students with special needs can reconnect with their sense of purpose, beat burnout, and achieve long-term success in their work.

By linking two key concepts in personal and professional development; that is, emotional intelligence and neuroplasticity, this guide offers a blueprint for building resilience, reducing stress, and enhancing emotional balance. The goal is not merely to *manage* existing challenges but to *transform* personal and professional practice so that special educators can thrive over the long term. In doing so, professionals create a positive ripple effect for students, colleagues, and school communities.

When special education professionals cultivate emotional intelligence, they develop a kind of internal scaffolding that allows them to navigate high-stress situations while remaining connected to their personal goals and val-ues. A landmark longitudinal study by Brackett et al. (2010) found that educators with higher levels of emotional intelligence reported significantly lower levels of emotional exhaustion and depersonalization, both key indi-cators of burnout. These educators were also more likely to experience job satisfaction and classroom effectiveness. Emotional regulation, in particular, emerged as a powerful buffer that helped educators maintain their well-being in high-pressure environments.[22]

The Prosocial Classroom framework, introduced by Jennings and Greenberg, confirms that teachers' social and emotional competence has far-reaching implications for school environments.[23] Their research shows that emotionally intelligent educators are more likely to foster supportive relationships with students, manage classrooms effectively, and reduce behavioral disruptions. These conditions enhance academic engagement and promote a more positive classroom climate. In short, emotionally competent educators are less vulnerable to stress-related burnout, making them more consistent and effective in their roles.

Further evidence comes from the Yale Center for Emotional Intelligence, whose RULER program has been adopted by thousands of schools across the United States and internationally. RULER is an acronym for Recognizing, Understanding, Labeling, Expressing, and Regulating emotions. The acronym equips educators and students with the language and tools to navigate emotional experiences constructively. Studies evaluating RULER schools show improvements in teacher retention, classroom climate, and student academic performance, along with significant reductions in teacher burnout and emotional fatigue.[24] These results reinforce a growing consensus in the field: Integrating emotional intelligence into daily practice is not an aspirational ideal. It is an evidence-based path toward resilience, renewal, and meaningful change.

When schools or districts prioritize their staff members' well-being and intentionally incorporate emotional intelligence training into professional development opportunities, the result is healthier school cultures and deeper relationships, setting the stage for educational systems where both students and staff can flourish.

Research by Elias and colleagues underscores that when schools adopt a coordinated approach to social-emotional learning that includes the explicit cultivation of emotional intelligence in staff, there are marked improvements in staff collaboration, leadership responsiveness, and the overall emotional climate of the school.[25] These shifts in adult behavior contribute directly to stronger student-teacher relationships and more effective instructional teams. Similarly, a study by Schonert-Reichl highlights that when schools integrate emotional-intelligence training into their professional-development curriculum, significant gains are apparent in organizational functioning and educator well-being. Teachers report greater confidence in handling conflict, improved communication with administrators, and a stronger sense of collective efficacy.[26]

Benefits of Integrating Emotional Intelligence
Individual and Systemic Outcomes

- Reduces emotional exhaustion, depersonalization, and burnout among special educators

- Improves job satisfaction and teacher retention

(Continued)

(Continued)

- Strengthens classroom management and reduces behavioral disruptions
- Enhances student-teacher relationships and classroom climate
- Increases academic engagement and student achievement
- Promotes collaboration, responsive leadership, and organizational well-being
- Builds educators' capacity to regulate emotions, handle conflict, and sustain resilience under pressure

Research clearly shows that the path forward is marked by tremendous possibility. Whether the tools in this book are used individually or systemically, once emotional intelligence becomes embedded in the daily practice of special educators, they are no longer left to rely on endurance alone. They gain access to tools that restore clarity, reconnect them to their purpose, and allow them to lead with compassion, even in the most complex settings.

NOTES

1. Maslach, C., & Leiter, M. P. (1997). *The truth about burnout: How organizations cause personal stress and what to do about it.* Jossey-Bass.

2. Freudenberger, H. (1974). Staff burn-out. *Journal of Social Issues, 30*(1), 159–65. doi:10.1111/j.1540-4560.1974.tb00706.x

3. Gallup. (2024, February 1). *Overworked and undervalued: Retaining top educators.* Gallup Education. https://www.gallup.com/education/

4. Gallup. (2022, June 13). K-12 Workers Have Highest Burnout Rate in U.S. https://news.gallup.com/poll/394895/k-12-workers-highest-burnout-rate.aspx.

5. Ingersoll, R., Merrill, L., & Stuckey, D. (2021, October). *Seven trends: The transformation of the teaching force.* Consortium for Policy Research in Education.

6. Billingsley, B., & Bettini, E. (2019). Special education teacher retention and attrition: A critical analysis of the literature. *Journal of Special Education, 53*(3), 151–63.

7. Bettini, E., & Gilmour, A. (2024, September). *Addressing special education staffing shortages: Strategies for schools.* EdResearch for Action Project: Annenberg Institute at Brown University; Results for America; Advancing Evidence. Improving Lives (AIR); Wheelock Educational Policy Center (WEPC). https://edresearchforaction.org/wp-content/uploads/55015-EdResearch-Special-Education-Staffing-Brief-31-FINAL-1-1.pdf

8. Office of Postsecondary Education, U.S. Department of Education. (2025). *Teacher shortage areas. Nationwide listing, 1990–1991 through 2024–25.* https://www.ed.gov/teaching-and-administration/professional-development/teacher-shortage-areas

9. American Speech-Language-Hearing Association. (n.d.) *Caseload and workload.* ASHA Practice Portal. https://www.asha.org/practice-portal/professional-issues/caseload-and-workload/

10. Spencer, K. C., Turkett, A., Vaughan, R., & Koenig, S. (2006). School-based practice patterns: A survey of occupational therapists in Colorado. *The American Journal of Occupational Therapy*, 60(1), 81–91. https://research.aota.org/ajot/article-abstract/60/1/81/28/School-Based-Practice-Patterns-A-Survey-of?redirectedFrom=fulltext; Stephenson, P. (2019, Mar.) Building resilience and minimizing burnout in school-based practice. *Journal of Occupational Therapy, Schools, & Early Intervention*, 12(3). https://www.tandfonline.com/doi/full/10.1080/19411243.2019.1590754

11. National Education Association (NEA). (2022). *NEA PreK–12 members: A closer look at support staff.* [Paraeducator Members]. https://www.nea.org/sites/default/files/2023-11/nea-paraeducatp-career-family-profile.pdf

12. Fisher, M., & Pleasants, S. L. (2011, Feb.). Roles, responsibilities, and concerns of paraeducators: Findings from a statewide survey. *Remedial and Special Education,* 33(5). https://doi.org/10.1177/0741932510397762

13. American School Counselor Association. (2023-24). *Student-to-School Counselor Ratio 2023–2024.* https://www.schoolcounselor.org/getmedia/f2a319d5-db73-4ca1-a515-2ad2c73ec746/Ratios-2023-24-Alpha.pdf

14. Carnes, S. L. (2023). Overworked and stretched thin: Burnout and systemic failure in school social work. *Children & Schools*, 45(3), 151–159. https://doi.org/10.1093/cs/cdad015

15. Plantiveau, C., Dounavi, K., & Virués-Ortega, J. (2018). Burnout in applied behavior analysis practitioners: a systematic review. *Journal of Autism and Developmental Disorders* 48(3), 1–14.

16. DeWitt, P. (2021, April). 42 percent of principals want to leave their position. Will you let them? *Education Week.* https://www.edweek.org/leadership/opinion-42-of-principals-want-to-leave-their-position-will-you-let-them/2021/04

17. U.S. Department of Education. (2024). *Teacher shortage areas.* https://www.ed.gov/teaching-and-administration/professional-development/teacher-shortage-areas

18. Billingsley, B., & Bettini, E. (2019). Special education teacher retention and attrition: A critical analysis of the literature. *Journal of Special Education,* 53(3), 151–63.

19. Gilmour, A., Mason-Williams, L., & Bettini, E. (n. d.). *How the special education teacher shortage affects students with LD and what to do about it.* Learning Disabilities Association of America. https://ldaamerica.org/how-the-special-education-teacher-shortage-affects-students-with-ld-and-what-to-do-about-it/

20. American Association of Colleges for Teacher Education. (2023). *Teacher education pipeline: The state of programs and enrollments 2023.* AACTE.

21. Office of Special Education Programs. (2024). *Annual report to Congress on the implementation of the individuals with disabilities Education Act 2023.* https://www.govinfo.gov/app/details/CMR-ED1-00187514

22. Brackett, M. A., Palomera, R., Mojsa-Kaja, J., Reyes, C. R., & Salovey, P. (2010). Emotion-regulation ability, burnout, and job satisfaction among British secondary-school teachers. *Psychology in the Schools, 47*(4), 406–17. doi:10.1002/pits.20478

23. Jennings, P. A., & Greenberg, M. T. (2009). The prosocial classroom: Teacher social and emotional competence in relation to student and classroom outcomes. *Review of Educational Research, 79*(1), 491–525. https://doi.org/10.3102/0034654308325693

24. Brackett, M. A., Rivers, S. E., Reyes, M. R., & Salovey, P. (2012). Enhancing academic performance and social and emotional competence with the RULER feeling words curriculum. *Learning and Individual Differences, 22*(2), 218–24. https://doi.org/10.1016/j.lindif.2010.10.002

25. Elias, M. J., O'Brien, M. U., & Weissberg, R. P. (2006, December). Transformative leadership for social and emotional learning. *Principal Leadership, 7*, 10–13. https://www.yumpu.com/en/document/view/11368550/transformative-leadership-for-social-emotional-learning-national-

26. Schonert-Reichl, K. A. (Spring 2017). Social and emotional learning and teachers. *Future of Children 27*(1), 137–55. doi:10.1353/foc.2017.0007

CHAPTER 2

Emotional Intelligence and Neuroplasticity

Between stimulus and response there is a space. In that space is our power to choose our response. In our response lies our growth and our freedom.

Attributed to Victor Frankl

Avoiding burnout and becoming the best at what you do begins with a clear understanding of change and how this process unfolds in the brain and body. The ultimate result of consistently using the tools in this book is growth through change, but change, even when beneficial, is not always comfortable. Furthermore, the tools provided here support *transformational* change, and that kind of change takes effort. It requires looking closely at habits and beliefs that may have served you in the past but no longer align with where you want to be. It takes patience, persistence, and a willingness to try, fail, and try again.

As you work through the strategies and tools in Part Two of this guide, you will notice a consistent focus on emotional intelligence and neuroplasticity. This is intentional. Both are fundamental to meaningful, lasting change.

Emotional intelligence and neuroplasticity interact within the brain's emotional and adaptive systems.[1] For example, Joseph LeDoux's research on the amygdala, a key part of the brain's emotional processing system, shows how your brain learns from experience and then shapes your reactions.[2] Think about a time when you reacted to stress by snapping at someone before you even had time to process what was happening. At that moment, your amygdala was running the show, taking what LeDoux describes as the emotional "low road."[3] This is the brain's automatic response system, bypassing rational thought in favor of instinct. But with conscious effort, you can train your brain to pause, giving yourself the space to respond with intention. That is neuroplasticity in action.[4]

When you choose to leverage neuroplasticity by actively increasing your emotional intelligence, you can successfully navigate emotions and relationships while building the resilience needed to mitigate stress.[5]

Before diving into the tools and strategies in Part II, it is essential to examine the foundation between them: the nature of emotional intelligence, the science of neuroplasticity, and how the two work together to drive meaningful change.

EMOTIONAL INTELLIGENCE

Emotional intelligence, a central concept in psychology and neuroscience, emerged from decades of research into human emotion, cognition, and behavior. The formal definition of emotional intelligence was first introduced by Peter Salovey and John D. Mayer in 1990. They describe it as "the ability to monitor one's own and others' feelings and emotions, to discriminate among them, and to use this information to guide one's thinking and actions."[6] At the time, intelligence was largely equated with cognitive ability (IQ), and emotional competencies were often overlooked. Their research shifted this understanding, demonstrating that emotional skills are critical for success, relationship building, and overall well-being.

Daniel Goleman later brought emotional intelligence into mainstream awareness.[7] Goleman expanded upon Salovey and Mayer's research, framing emotional intelligence as a practical framework for personal and professional life, particularly in the workplace and leadership settings. He introduced five key components of emotional intelligence: self-awareness, self-regulation, motivation, empathy, and social skills. His work emphasized that while cognitive intelligence is important, the ability to navigate emotions often plays an even more decisive role in achieving success and maintaining effective relationships.

Although Goleman's work made emotional intelligence widely accessible, its scientific foundations run deeper. Joseph LeDoux's research on the amygdala provided critical insight into how the brain processes intense emotions such as fear.[8] LeDoux identified two neural pathways for emotional responses: the "low road," a fast and instinctive reaction, and the "high road," a slower, more deliberate process that allows for thoughtful responses. His findings explain why emotional regulation requires effort and why building emotional intelligence demands conscious, sustained practice.

Since the publication of *Emotional Intelligence*, the original five-domain model has evolved into more detailed competency-based frameworks. In collaboration with Richard Boyatzis, Goleman helped develop a model that identifies twelve specific competencies grouped into four domains: self-awareness, self-management, social awareness, and relationship management.[9] This competency-based structure is now widely used in leadership development, executive coaching, education, and healthcare training, and serves as the foundation for tools such as the Emotional and Social Competency Inventory.

Although newer models offer greater specificity in applied settings, the original five-domain framework—self-awareness, self-regulation, motivation, empathy, and social skills—continues to serve a vital role in education, psychology, and social-emotional learning initiatives. It remains widely referenced in research literature, professional training programs, and organizational development initiatives. Organizations such as the Collaborative for Academic, Social, and Emotional Learning (CASEL) and the Yale Center for Emotional Intelligence (YCEI) adapt and build upon the five-domain model to inform evidence-based programs, curriculum development, and educator training.[10]

This book uses the original five-domain framework because of its clarity, accessibility, and enduring relevance across disciplines. Dividing emotional intelligence into self-awareness, self-regulation, motivation, empathy, and social skills offers a structure that supports targeted skill development and practical application. While competency-based models are well-suited for corporate leadership development, the five-domain model remains particularly effective for educational, clinical, and social-emotional contexts. Its language is familiar to practitioners, its categories are easily understood by diverse audiences, and it creates a direct link between research, intervention strategies, and real-world outcomes.

NEUROPLASTICITY

Neuroplasticity is the brain's remarkable ability to adapt, reorganize, and even rewire itself in response to experiences, learning, and behavior. In short, our brains are constantly changing.

The idea of neuroplasticity has been around for more than a century, but for much of that time, scientists believed the brain became fixed after childhood. This meant that if you did not develop certain skills within a specific timeframe during childhood, those skills could never be regained. Decades of research have since overturned that belief. Scientists like Michael Merzenich, Paul Bach-y-Rita, and Eric Kandel have shown that the brain remains adaptable throughout life, constantly forming new connections and pathways in response to practice, repetition, and even conscious effort.[11]

Neuroplasticity operates structurally and functionally. Structurally, it reshapes neural networks in the brain, forming new connections that strengthen with consistent practice. Functionally, neuroplasticity is what allows different parts of the brain to take over when needed, such as after an injury or when compensating for lost skills. In either case, the brain is not static. It is a dynamic system that responds directly to how you think, act, and engage with your environment.

Emotional intelligence is about how we perceive, manage, and influence emotions. Neuroplasticity is what makes it possible to develop and strengthen those abilities. Imagine your brain as a network of pathways. Every time you practice empathy, self-awareness, or emotional regulation, you are carving out new paths or reinforcing the ones that already exist. With enough repetition, these skills become second nature because the brain has rewired itself to make them easier.[12]

CONNECTING EI AND NEUROPLASTICITY

Emotional intelligence and neuroplasticity are not just connected; they actively shape one another. Every time you regulate an emotional reaction, pause before responding impulsively, or choose to practice empathy, you leverage neuroplasticity and strengthen the neural pathways that make those skills more accessible.[13]

The amygdala, often described as the brain's emotional alarm system, plays a key role in processing emotions and triggering automatic reactions in moments of stress.[14] When emotions take over, the brain falls back to well-established neural pathways to determine a response. If someone has a habit of reacting to stress with frustration or avoidance, those responses become more ingrained. An example of this could be a special educator who, after months of working with a student who frequently yells and throws his stress ball in her direction, develops an automatic stress response as soon as the student picks up the stress ball. Reacting from the "low road," she may raise her voice and immediately move to retrieve the object, even if the student had no intention of throwing it. The low road, a fast and instinctive response driven by the amygdala, is useful in moments that require immediate action, but defaulting to these familiar patterns reinforces reactive emotional responses that may not match the situation or support your desired outcome.

When you consciously work to develop your emotional intelligence, the prefrontal cortex—the area responsible for rational thinking, impulse control, and long-term decision-making—becomes more engaged.[15] The tools and strategies in Part II are designed to strengthen this area of the brain and support the regulation of your amygdala's emotional responses. This allows for a more balanced and deliberate way of processing emotions and responding with intention. With consistent practice, reactivity fades, and decisions are made from a place of clarity and composure.

The connection between EI and neuroplasticity is both simple and amazing. When you use a tool or technique to develop an EI domain, your brain's neuroplasticity supports your choice by rewiring your neural networks to access LeDoux's high road. The more you practice, the more you reinforce your route to the high road, allowing it to become your effortless default. By choosing to develop your emotional intelligence, you are choosing to build neural pathways that support you in countless ways. Your stress, negative emotions, and fatigue decrease while your confidence, composure, resilience, motivation, and well-being increase. This allows you to show up as your best self, even in the most challenging situations.

NOTES

1. Siegel, D. J. (2020). *The developing mind: How relationships and the brain interact to shape who we are* (3rd ed.). Guilford Press.

2. LeDoux, J. (1996). *The emotional brain: The mysterious underpinnings of emotional life.* Simon & Schuster.

3. LeDoux, J. (2002). *Synaptic self: How our brains become who we are.* Viking.

4. Merzenich, M. M. (2013). *Soft-wired: How the new science of brain plasticity can change your life.* Parnassus.

5. Goleman, D. (1998). *Working with emotional intelligence.* Bantam Books.

6. Salovey, P., & Mayer, J. D. (1990) Emotional intelligence. *Imagination, Cognition and Personality 9*(3), 185–211. https://doi.org/10.2190/DUGG-P24E-52WK-6CDG

7. Goleman, D. (1995). *Emotional intelligence: Why it can matter more than IQ.* Bantam Books.

8. LeDoux, J. (2015). *Anxious: Using the brain to understand and treat fear and anxiety.* Viking.

9. Goleman, D., & Boyatzis, R. E. (2017). *Emotional and social competency inventory: Technical manual.* Hay Group.

10. Collaborative for Academic, Social, and Emotional Learning. (2023) *SEL framework.* CASEL. https://casel.org/what-is-sel/

11. Merzenich, M. M. *Soft-wired*; Valk, S. L., Kanske, P., Park, B. Y., Hong, S. J., Böckler, A., Trautwein, F. M., Bernhardt, B. C., & Singer, T. (2023, July 7). *Functional and microstructural plasticity following social and interoceptive mental training.* eLife. https://doi.org/10.7554/eLife.85188; Kandel, E. R. (2012). *The age of insight: the quest to understand the unconscious in art, mind, and brain.* Random House.

12. Merzenich, M. M. *Soft-wired*; Valk, S. L., Kanske, P., Park, B. Y., Hong, S. J., Böckler, A., Trautwein, F. M., Bernhardt, B. C., & Singer, T. (2023, July 7). *Functional and microstructural plasticity following social and interoceptive mental training.* eLife. https://doi.org/10.7554/eLife.85188;

13. Kandel, E. R. (2012). *The age of insight: the quest to understand the unconscious in art, mind, and brain.* Random House.

14. LeDoux, J. (2012). Rethinking the emotional brain. *Neuron, 73*(4), 653–676. doi: 10.1016/j.neuron.2012.02.004

15. Squire, L. R., & Kandel, E. R. (2009). *Memory: From mind to molecules* (2nd ed.). W. H. Freeman.

CHAPTER 3

Transformational Tools: Structure and Function

I knew how to teach, how to plan, and how to structure a classroom for students with special needs, but no one ever taught me how to handle the stress and emotions that come with this work.

S. Collins, Special Education Teacher

Now more than ever, special educators need skills beyond technical expertise to manage the emotional and cognitive load that comes with their work. A good education, experience, and a strong professional skill set can set the stage for success, but to thrive and excel in your role, superior emotional intelligence skills are a must.[1]

This chapter explains how the tools to develop your emotional intelligence are organized and presented throughout the rest of the book. It also details how each tool works to interrupt patterns that do not support your growth, while forming new patterns that do. This understanding is essential because emotional intelligence is not static. Through consistent practice, your skills refine and strengthen over time.

EMOTIONAL INTELLIGENCE DOMAINS

Figure 3.1 outlines the five domains of emotional intelligence discussed in chapter 2: self-awareness, self-regulation, motivation, empathy, and social skills. Each domain plays a distinct role, but together, they serve as the organizing framework for this book, shaping the structure of the tools and guiding their application. As shown in Figure 3.1, the domains are grouped into two categories: internal and external. Self-awareness, self-regulation, and motivation fall under *internal* domains because they center on your personal growth and lived experience. Empathy and social skills are *external* factors governing how you connect and communicate with others. Technically, you can develop emotional intelligence skills by approaching the domains in any order, but research consistently shows that beginning with the internal domains lays a stronger foundation for the successful development of external domains.[2]

FIGURE 3.1 Five Domains of Emotional Intelligence

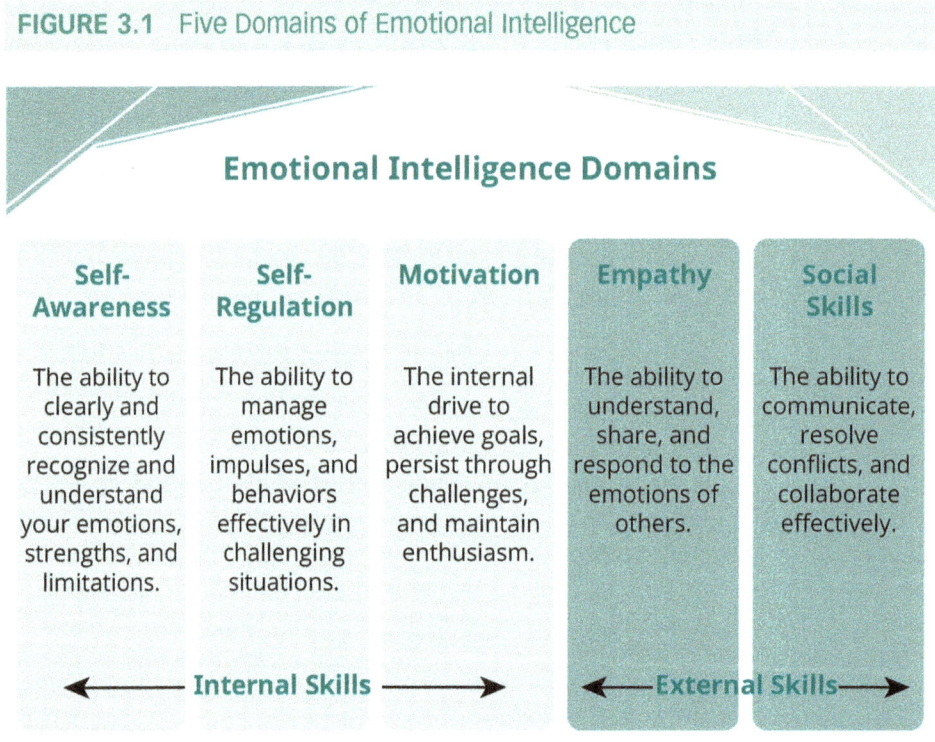

Studies indicate that individuals with strong self-awareness and self-regulation are better equipped to manage interpersonal relationships effectively.[3] Without internal mastery, external emotional intelligence skills such as empathy and social skills can be inconsistent and reactive rather than intentional.[4] Repeated practice in self-awareness and self-regulation strengthens areas in the brain that govern impulse control, emotional regulation, and problem-solving (prefrontal cortex).[5] Figure 3.2 illustrates that strengthening internal tools forms the roots that grow into outward-facing skills.

FIGURE 3.2 Internal and External EI Development

Like a tree, mastery of emotional intelligence skills begins with a strong foundation. Roots provide the stability needed to grow and thrive, just like the internal competencies of motivation, self-awareness, and self-regulation. Once the roots are strong, external skills can develop, allowing individuals to engage effectively with the world.

To best align with research, this book takes a neuroscience-informed approach by providing more depth and attention to the chapters on self-awareness, self-regulation, and motivation. These chapters offer deeper exploration and more opportunities for reflection. Once internal skills become second nature, outward-facing skills such as empathy and social awareness come more naturally and with greater authenticity.

Now that we have discussed how the tools are structured and the best approach to mastery within the emotional intelligence framework, we need to examine the function of the tools, or how change happens in the brain.

THE NEUROSCIENCE OF EMOTIONAL RESPONSES

Professionals who work with children or adults with special needs face unpredictable situations regularly. Over time, these emotions may become linked with particular individuals, settings, or even times of the day. For example, a school administrator forcibly pushed aside by a student threatening to fight a peer might experience sudden anxiety when the student approaches him the next day, even if the student presents a calm demeanor. Similarly, if you are a special education teacher and your class regularly becomes loud and chaotic before lunch, you may feel frustrated close to lunchtime, even on quieter days.

Neuroscientist Joseph LeDoux explains that the brain's defense system is wired for survival, and this is why reactive emotions can become linked to specific situations.[6] When your brain perceives a threat, whether physical or emotional, it rapidly forms neural connections to trigger a protective response that prepares you for defensive or offensive action. In a classroom setting, this often results in your brain unconsciously associating certain students or environments with stress, even when no immediate threat exists.

This pattern emerges not only in moments of extreme stress. It can develop in the daily routines of educators as well. Consider a teacher balancing lesson planning, student behaviors, administrative demands, and the pressure to meet the needs of a diverse classroom. Over time, the *accumulation* of stress can trigger irritability or anxiety in response to the classroom setting itself. If these patterns continue, the brain links everyday teaching challenges with stress and exhaustion, and this makes it harder to approach situations with clarity and patience.

Consistently using the tools in this book can change things for the better by forming new feedback loops in the brain that serve you. This is because your brain's neuroplasticity allows for the formation of new neural networks that increase resilience, clarity, and control in high-stress situations[7] through an *adaptive feedback loop*. However, when certain situations repeatedly trigger frustration or anxiety, they create *maladaptive feedback loops*. These patterns of reaction become deeply ingrained, making emotional regulation more difficult, as noted in Figure 3.3.

Imagine you associate morning coffee with starting your workday. The coffee makes you feel awake and alert, ready for the tasks ahead. Over time, just the smell of coffee can make you feel attentive and engaged. This is an example of a feedback loop—your brain strengthens connections between repeated experiences (morning coffee) and automatic responses (alertness). The more often an emotion or reaction occurs, the more automatic it becomes. Some feedback loops help us adapt, while others reinforce stress-based reactions, and many, like the morning coffee example, remain somewhat neutral.

FIGURE 3.3 Adaptive and Maladaptive Feedback Loops

Adaptive Feedback Loop

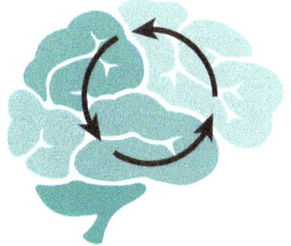

Strengthens positive emotional regulation, resilience, and intentional responses. With repeated practice, neural pathways supporting self-awareness, emotional control, and cognitive flexibility become stronger, making it easier to respond with clarity and composure.

Maladaptive Feedback Loop

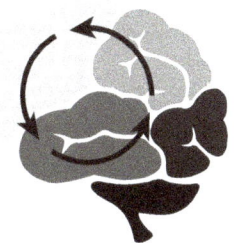

Reinforces emotional patterns that undermine emotional regulation like chronic stress, frustration, defensive reactions. The brain strengthens these pathways over time, making responses automatic. Shifting toward more regulated responses requires focused effort.

The brain does not inherently judge whether a feedback loop is good or bad. What makes a loop adaptive or maladaptive depends on whether it helps or harms you. If a loop supports your well-being and goals, it serves you in a positive way. If it keeps you stuck in distress or unhelpful patterns, it works against you. The brain reinforces either pattern in the same way, and this gives you the power to change maladaptive loops by intentionally practicing new, more supportive patterns until they become your default.

While all feedback loops strengthen neural pathways, they can be shaped by external reinforcement or by internal emotional and cognitive patterns. External feedback loops develop through outside influences, such as rewards and consequences, while internal loops emerge from personal thoughts, emotions, and repeated experiences. Recognizing this distinction is essential for understanding how emotional intelligence tools reshape automatic responses.

Feedback Loops: External Reinforcement

Most special educators understand feedback loops through tools like positive behavior supports and token economy systems, which create adaptive feedback loops for your students. For example, when a student receives tokens for staying on task, the brain strengthens neural pathways that link effort with positive reinforcement. This forms an adaptive feedback loop, which increases the likelihood that the desired behavior will repeat in different settings.

Conversely, if a staff member frequently removes a student from class when he is disruptive, the temporary relief from a challenging task activates stress-reducing neural pathways. Over time, the student learns that outbursts lead to escape, reinforcing a maladaptive feedback loop. This makes the student more likely to continue using disruptive behavior to avoid difficult tasks.

These feedback loops are relatively straightforward: A response follows a behavior that either reinforces or discourages it.

Feedback Loops: Internal Patterns

Although external reinforcement plays an important role in behavioral conditioning, this book focuses on the *internal*, automatic feedback loops developed through accumulated stress, patterned emotional reactions, and the brain's tendency to anticipate and prepare for real or perceived threats.

Internal patterns created from stress responses are not conscious choices. They are automatic reactions developed through repeated exposure to situational stress. The tools in this guide leverage the fact that internal feedback loops can also develop from positive experiences. When someone repeatedly experiences success, composure, focus, or a sense of competence, the brain strengthens neural pathways that reinforce confidence and emotional resilience.[8] The three examples in Table 3.1 invite you to contrast maladaptive and adaptive responses in identical situations.

TABLE 3.1   Examples of Adaptive and Maladaptive Responses

SCENARIO	MALADAPTIVE RESPONSE	ADAPTIVE RESPONSE
A student frequently has aggressive outbursts in class.	As soon as the student walks into the classroom, his teacher feels tension and stress regardless of the student's mood and behavior.	As soon as the student walks into the classroom, his teacher begins belly breathing and feels a steady sense of calm. This allows her to focus on the present moment rather than past incidents and observe the student objectively.
A school social worker is typically met with hostility by a student's parents.	The social worker finds her heart racing and palms sweating before sitting down for an IEP discussion.	The social worker feels grounded as she sits down for an IEP discussion because she regularly engages in perspective taking exercises and does not take the parents' hostility personally. She understands that from their perspective, the parents are deeply worried that their child will not develop the skills needed to live independently.

SCENARIO	MALADAPTIVE RESPONSE	ADAPTIVE RESPONSE
A paraprofessional is frequently called to physically intervene in intense student crises	When students raise their voices or show frustration, the paraprofessional instinctively tightens his muscles, bracing for a potential escalation.	When students raise their voices or show frustration, the paraprofessional practices box breathing. He remains centered and calm, which allows him to effectively observe students' behaviors objectively.

The solutions provided in this book provide the opportunity for you to develop and strengthen adaptive feedback loops so that they become your default, automatic responses to stress, overwhelm, and exhaustion.

TRANSFORMATIVE TOOLS: WHAT TO EXPECT

Part Two is organized around the five domains of emotional intelligence: self-awareness, self-regulation, motivation, empathy, and social skills. Each internal domain is supported by two chapters that are designed to work together. The first chapter in each pair offers foundational insight, research, and context. They explain what the tools do and why they work. The second provides the usable tools and strategies for real-world application:

- Chapters 4 and 5 focus on self-awareness.

- Chapters 6 and 7 explore self-regulation.

- Chapters 8 and 9 cover internal motivation.

Chapter 10 brings the three internal domains together by presenting daily and situational scenarios that combine the tools from chapters 5, 7, and 9. This chapter demonstrates how internal strategies work in harmony and shows how developing them together can accelerate growth in practical and sustainable ways.

Chapter 11 introduces the two external emotional intelligence domains: empathy and social skills. This chapter explains how the external tools work and the research that supports why they work. Chapter 12 provides tools and strategies for developing empathy, and Chapter 13 offers practical tools for developing social skills.

All "tools" chapters (5, 7, 9, 12, and 13) follow a consistent structure:

- Each tool includes a list of research-based techniques that guide its implementation and practice in both personal and professional settings.

- Each tool includes a list of current technology options (if available) to support the effective use of the tool and strategies.

- One to two real-world examples illustrate how special education professionals can integrate the tools and strategies into their daily professional lives, showing their relevance in special education contexts.

- Following real-world scenarios, a section called *Key Considerations* highlights important takeaways and the neuroscience and research behind each tool.

As you read through the following chapters, take a moment to reflect on which domain of emotional intelligence you need to strengthen first. Consider starting with one or two foundational strategies: self-awareness, self-regulation, or motivation that best aligns with your current needs and professional setting, and commit to practicing them regularly. Remember that change takes time. The brain needs repetition to form new pathways. As you engage with these tools and techniques, reflect on your experiences and note any changes in your emotional awareness, regulation, and overall resilience.

There is no single way to approach this work. Some professionals may find that one strategy is enough, while others may prefer to combine multiple approaches. Some may gravitate toward technology-based tools, while others may select more traditional methods. The key is to allow yourself flexibility in how you apply the strategies so that they blend easily into your work environment. Different situations may require different strategies, and what works well in one setting may need adjustment in another. No matter how you choose to approach this work, remember, you are investing in your long-term well-being and professional effectiveness.

NOTES

1. Goleman, D. (1995). *Emotional intelligence: Why it can matter more than IQ*. Bantam, 43–45.

2. Jennings, P. A., & Greenberg, M. T. (2009). The prosocial classroom: Teacher social and emotional competence in relation to student and classroom outcomes. *Review of Educational Research, 79*(1), 491–525. https://doi.org/10.3102/0034654308325693

3. Bradberry, T., & Greaves, J. (2009). *Emotional intelligence 2.0*. TalentSmart, 19–21.

4. Bradberry, T., & Greaves, J. (2009). *Emotional intelligence 2.0*. TalentSmart, 46–48.

5. Merzenich, M. M. (2013). *Soft-wired: How the new science of brain plasticity can change your life*. Parnassus, 101–5.

6. LeDoux, J. E. (1996). *The emotional brain: The mysterious underpinnings of emotional life*. Simon & Schuster, 162–68.

7. Doidge, N. (2007). *The brain that changes itself: Stories of personal triumph from the frontiers of brain science*. Viking, 210–15.

8. Doidge, N. (2007). *The brain that changes itself: Stories of personal triumph from the frontiers of brain science*. Viking, 257–59.

PART 2

Transformative Tools and Strategies

CHAPTER 4

Developing Self-Awareness

Have you ever been caught off guard by a sudden wave of frustration? Let's say your supervisor added new tasks to your workload when you were already stretched thin, and before you fully registered what was happening, your temperature spiked, and your thoughts raced. Then you reacted. You raised your voice in protest, grabbed your belongings, and stormed out of the room. Moments like these show how quickly emotions can take the wheel, steering our behavior before we realize it. When that happens, embarrassment usually follows, and the problem remains unaddressed and unresolved.

While self-awareness may seem like a natural ability, it is a skill that requires practice. Many people go through their day without noticing their emotional states or the "triggers" that influence their reactions. In high-stress environments, emotions can surface so quickly that they feel automatic, leaving you wondering, "Where did that come from?" Developing self-awareness helps bring these underlying patterns into focus, allowing for more deliberate responses.

WHAT SELF-AWARENESS TOOLS DO

Self-awareness tools help you recognize and identify your emotions while providing insight into what causes them. These insights can diffuse the intensity of your emotions and create the clarity needed to respond with intention. When emotions rise quickly and feel automatic, self-awareness strategies allow you to observe what is beneath the surface before emotions shape your behavior.

Imagine you are in a staff meeting, and you feel your jaw tighten, your shoulders lift, and your stomach turn. Without self-awareness, you might ignore these signals, or maybe react without understanding their origin. But if you choose to use a self-awareness tool in that moment, you can pause and observe what your body is telling you. Then you might name the emotion. Perhaps it is anger, confusion, or resentment. By naming it, you bring the experience into conscious awareness and interrupt the automatic loop that would otherwise intensify your emotional state. This allows you to choose a response that serves you.

Self-awareness is more than being informed about your internal experience as it unfolds. It also reveals a clear understanding of your emotional triggers. When you are clear on what words, circumstances, tasks, or even gestures elicit a strong emotional reaction, those triggers lose their power to create automatic emotional responses, and this creates a critical shift. Instead of being caught off guard by an emotion, you can identify where friction is likely to occur, anticipate how specific situations might affect you, and prepare to respond with intention rather than instinct. You can operate from a place of clarity and agency, which allows you to remain steady and responsive, even when the pressure around you begins to build.

WHY SELF-AWARENESS TOOLS WORK

Studies show that identifying and labeling emotions helps reduce activity in the amygdala,[1] the region in your brain responsible for reactive responses. At the same time, naming your feelings activates the prefrontal cortex,[2] which supports thoughtful decision-making. This shift allows you to override automatic reactions and regulate your emotions more effectively so that you can approach challenges with greater clarity and emotional stability.

Tools and practices that cultivate self-awareness create structural changes in the brain. For example, Britta K. Hölzel and colleagues found that regular mindfulness (a self-awareness tool) increases gray matter density in brain regions associated with self-awareness and emotional resilience, including the prefrontal cortex and hippocampus.[3] These changes enhance an individual's ability to recognize and regulate emotions in high-stress environments.

Joseph LeDoux's work on emotional processing further emphasizes that self-awareness allows the brain to override defensive responses and form healthier neural connections.[4] When you begin to understand what triggers your emotional reactions, you are better able to interrupt automatic stress responses and choose more intentional ways of engaging in challenges.

QUICK SUMMARY

Self-awareness tools do more than provide a momentary sense of control. They train you to observe without reacting, to recognize patterns, and to shift your responses in real time. When you take charge of your emotional triggers, you gain the power to stop escalation before it starts, to stay focused when tension rises, and to respond with clarity instead of being pulled into the emotional intensity around you. The next chapter provides six tools to help you develop this important skill, along with a variety of techniques (with and without technology) to support implementation.

Reflections

Think of an incident or circumstance when you reacted before thinking and consider the following questions.

1. What physical sensations did you notice in your body before, during, or immediately after your reaction? Consider changes in muscle tension, breathing, temperature, posture, or any other bodily responses. How might these physical signals serve as early warning indicators in future situations?

_____

_____

_____

_____

_____

_____

2. Can you identify and name the specific emotions you experienced? Move beyond broad categories like "angry" or "upset." Were you frustrated, betrayed, overwhelmed, disrespected, anxious, or something else? List two to three emotions that capture the complexity of what you felt.

_____

_____

_____

_____

_____

_____

(Continued)

(Continued)

3. What external factors may have made you more susceptible to reacting automatically in this situation? Consider your stress level, fatigue, workload, recent events, time of day, or other circumstances that might have lowered your emotional resilience in that moment.

_____

_____

_____

_____

_____

_____

NOTES

1. Lieberman, M. D., Eisenberger, N. I., Crockett, M. J., Tom, S. M., Pfeifer, J. H., & Way, B. M. (2007). Putting feelings into words: Affect labeling disrupts amygdala activity in response to affective stimuli. *Psychological Science, 18*(5), 421–28. https://doi.org/10.1111/j.1467-9280.2007.01916.x

2. Lazar, S. W., Kerr, C. E., Wasserman, R. H., Gray, J. R., Greve, D. N., Treadway, M. T., McGarvey, M., Quinn, B. T., Dusek, J. A., Benson, H., Rauch, S. L., Moore, C. I., & Fischl, B. (2005). Meditation experience is associated with increased cortical thickness. *NeuroReport, 16*(17), 1893–97. DOI: 10.1097/01.wnr.0000186598.66243.19

3. Hölzel, B. K., Carmody, J., Vangel. M., Congleton, C., Yerramsetti, S. M., Gard, T., & Lazar, S. W. (2011). Mindfulness practice leads to increases in regional brain gray matter density. *Psychiatry Research: Neuroimaging, 191*(1), 36–43. https://doi.org/10.1016/j.pscychresns.2010.08.006

4. LeDoux, J. (2012). Rethinking the emotional brain. *Neuron, 73*(4), 653–76. https://doi.org/10.1016/j.neuron.2012.02.004

CHAPTER 5

Self-Awareness Tools

Self-awareness is often described as the cornerstone of emotional intelligence. When you are aware of your emotional state, you can pause before reacting, and that pause creates space for choice. Without self-awareness, you are more likely to say something regrettable, misinterpret someone else's behavior, or take action that is not aligned with your values.

Emotional intelligence domains like self-regulation become nearly impossible without self-awareness skills because you cannot manage what you have not yet noticed and identified. Cultivating external skills like empathy and social competence relies on self-awareness as a starting point. When you are aware of your emotional states, you become more attuned to the emotional experiences of others. You know when your feelings are distorting how you see someone else, or when your discomfort is making you impatient or avoidant. Developing self-awareness skills gives you an internal compass that keeps the rest of your emotional intelligence skills aligned.

There are a multitude of available strategies designed to help you better understand your thoughts, emotions, and reactions, but this chapter narrows the focus to six research-backed tools and supporting techniques: reflective journaling, body scanning, mindfulness, gratitude practices, expressive writing, and affect labeling. Each tool is selected for its proven impact and practicality in the fast-paced, emotionally demanding environments where special educators, leaders, and mental health professionals operate. Figure 5.1 gives a very brief overview of the selected tools for this chapter.

Whether you are seeking a daily practice or an occasional outlet for processing emotions, these tools offer a versatile and powerful starting point.

FIGURE 5.1 Self-Awareness Tools

SELECTED TOOLS FOR SELF-AWARENESS

Reflective Journaling

Reflective writing allows you to recognize and understand emotional patterns and triggers, which gives you the power to make intentional adjustments that serve your well-being.

Body Scanning

Body scanning is a guided practice that involves mentally scanning the body to notice tension, discomfort, or other sensations so that you can mitigate stress before it intensifies.

Mindfulness

Mindfulness practices involve focusing your attention on the present moment so that you stay grounded and intentional in your responses.

Gratitude Practices

Gratitude practices shift your attention from reactive states to constructive emotions, enhancing awareness of your emotional baseline.

Expressive Writing

Writing without judgment or analysis helps you process and release deeper emotions resulting in a sense of release and calm.

Affect Labeling

Affect labeling is a process of specifically naming your emotions, which brings an immediate shift from reactivity to conscious consideration.

REFLECTIVE JOURNALING

Tool Number One: Reflective Journaling

I know what you might be thinking. "Who has time for journaling?" Given the nonstop demands of your day, pausing to reflect and journal might seem impractical, and just one more thing to fit in. But research underscores the power of structured reflection through journaling. This practice enhances your resilience and strengthens your mental flexibility.[1] Reflective journaling is not concerned with venting or tracking your daily events. It involves specific techniques that activate your neural pathways so that you can recognize patterns in your reactions, giving you the insights to make intentional adjustments. Just a few minutes of structured journaling can reduce your stress significantly.[2] Over time, this practice can transform how you engage with challenges, shifting from reaction to response.

If journaling is simply not a practice you can see yourself doing, don't worry; there are plenty of other options to develop self-awareness throughout this chapter. But if you are willing to give this tool a try, the following techniques will help structure your entries so that you can recognize your emotional patterns and pinpoint the triggers that cause them.

Techniques for Reflective Journaling

Select Columns

Divide your page into sections for selected events, emotions, and lessons learned, and complete each column. The content can be simple, bulleted points, or extensive narrative descriptions.

Scenarios

Write a detailed scenario of a selected event that caused your emotional reaction. Then, try to determine exactly which part(s) of the scenario triggered the emotion. Was it a word or a phrase? The person's body language? A look or a gesture? Journal your thoughts on the trigger *and* the associated emotion.

Cause-and-effect

Create a cause-and-effect diagram of selected scenarios that elicit emotional responses. Try to target the cause and effect as specifically as you can. For example, instead of writing the cause as "Jamie was rude," and the effect as "I was upset," consider adding details like "Jamie dismissed my ideas, and her tone was condescending. That triggered feelings of insecurity, which made me angry and defensive."

The goal is to unpack both the external trigger and your internal interpretation, so you can better understand the full emotional sequence. This level of detail strengthens emotional insight and helps you identify patterns in your reactions and the narratives you construct around difficult moments.

Color-coding

This technique is extremely helpful for identifying recurring emotions and the patterns that elicit them. When journaling, use color-coding to assign different colors with specific emotions to make patterns easier to identify. For example, angry could be marked with a yellow highlight, overwhelmed could be identified with a green highlight, and proud might show a pink highlight.

Regularly review your journal, noticing the patterns through the color coding. Over time, this visual tracking can help you recognize emotional triggers, understand how certain environments or interactions affect your mood, and build greater self-awareness around your internal responses. It also allows you to see emotional growth, revealing where regulation strategies are working and where further support might be needed.

1. Create a daily habit of adding to your notebook. This can be before the workday starts, at the end of the day, or before going to bed.

2. At the end of each week, create an index of key emotions, lessons learned, or key insights for quick reference.

3. Remember to include scenarios that made you feel happiness, joy, or other positive emotions. Self-awareness is not just knowing what triggers you but also what makes you happy and why!

Implementing Reflective Journaling

Mr. Michaels

Mr. Michaels, a school counselor, froze as a student with a history of trauma and a diagnosis of ADHD threw a chair in his direction. It happened right after he asked the student how he was feeling. His heart raced, and he immediately called for support.

During his lunch break, Mr. Michaels opened his reflective journal. He uses the Scenario format and color-coded emotions to track patterns. He wrote: "Student became aggressive when I asked a simple question. I felt overwhelmed (yellow highlight) and fearful (lavender highlight), then incompetent (light green highlight) when I called for help immediately instead of trying to de-escalate the student."

While journaling, Mr. Michaels began to focus on his feelings of overwhelm and fear, thinking about when those feelings actually began. It was before the chair was thrown, when the student entered the room with his fists clenched. When he reviewed the yellow and lavender highlights throughout his journal, almost all were related to a student's anger and corresponding body language.

Mr. Michaels scanned the dates of his entries and realized that this pattern had developed shortly after a colleague had been injured by a student in crisis earlier in the school year. Because of that incident, his threshold for calling support had lowered significantly, and this triggered feelings of incompetence because he knew that he had the skills to attempt de-escalation, but he was reacting from a place of fear and self-protection.

By gaining a deeper understanding of his feelings and responses, Mr. Michaels entered future student sessions with greater self-awareness. When a student entered his room angry, he could now take a breath and assess the potential danger more clearly and objectively. This allowed him to access his professional skills, bypassing the automatic fear response that developed from a traumatic event.

Key Considerations: Mr. Michaels

Mr. Michaels's experience shows how reflective journaling strengthens self-awareness by uncovering patterns in emotional responses. His color-coded entries helped him recognize that his fear and feelings of incompetence weren't just about individual student incidents. They were tied to unprocessed trauma from his colleague's injury earlier in the year. By stepping back and analyzing his reactions through journaling, he noticed a key pattern: His emotional responses were being triggered by angry body language, which activated his fear-based protective responses rather than his professional de-escalation skills.

This kind of reflection can change the way the brain processes stress. By regularly writing about his experiences and tracing his emotions back to their source, Mr. Michaels strengthens the brain's ability to slow down, recognize when past trauma is influencing present responses, and access his professional skills rather than reacting from fear.

Technological Options for Reflective Journaling

Notion is a versatile platform for organizing thoughts and reflections, offering customizable templates and multimedia integration.

Google Docs and *Microsoft Word* offer simple, cloud-based tools for writing and storing reflective entries, with collaborative options.

Daylio combines mood tracking with journaling, offering insights through visual statistics and patterns.

Journey is a polished journaling app with prompts, multimedia features, and cross-device syncing.

Reflectly, a guided journaling app using AI, offers personalized prompts and motivational notifications.

Otter.ai and *Google Keep* convert spoken reflections into text, ideal for on-the-go journaling and voice-to-text convenience.

Evernote combines text, images, and audio in journal entries, with robust tagging and search capabilities.

Implementing Reflective Journaling With Technology

Ms. Levy

Ms. Levy, a middle school special education teacher, uses the Daylio app for daily reflections. Transitioning from the small group classroom to the gym is often challenging, but today a student refused to line up when the bell rang. This resulted in students becoming highly agitated, and Ms. Levy raised her voice in frustration, telling the student to, "Line up right now or you will have silent lunch tomorrow!" The student responded by arguing, which prolonged both his and his peer's departures and increased Ms. Levy's frustration to the point of overwhelm. By the time the student complied, the class had lost fifteen minutes of their gym time, and Ms. Levy lost that time to plan and reset.

While her students were in the gym, Ms. Levy journaled about the incident, writing "Frustrated" and "Overwhelmed" in the Daylio app.

As Ms. Levy reviewed previous entries, she noticed a clear pattern: Transition periods consistently triggered frustration and feelings of overwhelm for her. These feelings weren't tied to specific students but to classroom dynamics during transition times. Digging deeper, she realized her emotional state often mirrored her students' dysregulation just before major changes or transitions. Because her nervous system was already heightened close to transition times, any issues with students quickly brought on feelings of frustration or overwhelm.

Based on this insight, Ms. Levy gained the clarity needed to develop a new approach to transitions both for herself and her students. She now sets a timer for three minutes before major transitions and begins belly breathing, a self-regulation strategy, for thirty seconds. Then she leads the class in a calming sensory activity that she actively participates in. This approach opens the possibility of shifting the dysregulation typically associated with transitions to a more balanced emotional climate for herself and her students.

Key Considerations: Ms. Levy

Ms. Levy's experience highlights how reflective journaling enhances self-awareness by revealing patterns in emotional responses rather than viewing them as isolated reactions. Research on student teachers within an educational environment showed that reflective journaling increases self-awareness and facilitates higher-order skills like critical thinking, reflection, and problem solving.[3]

By documenting her reflections, Ms. Levy moves beyond surface-level frustrations and gains insight from a much broader perspective. From there, she can proactively address the issue by creating a solid plan of action that can shift transition dynamics over time.

BODY SCANNING

Tool Number Two: Body Scanning

The introduction to chapter 4 illustrates how emotions tied to stress can manifest in your body before you are even aware of them. The body detects stress before the mind fully processes it, and this happens because the brain and nervous system are constantly scanning for potential threats.[4] As a result, your shoulders might tense, your stomach might clench, or your breathing might change suddenly, and without your awareness. By consciously connecting your body and emotions through regular check-ins, you can identify and handle stress before it escalates.

Body scanning is a mindfulness practice that brings deliberate attention to physical sensations throughout the body. The next section of this chapter will focus extensively on mindfulness as a tool, but body scanning stands out as a foundational practice and is included here as a separate tool because it focuses on concrete, somatic awareness rather than abstract mental processes. This tangible approach makes body scanning particularly effective for people who prefer sensation-based practices over thought-focused mindfulness techniques.

Before sharing specific techniques for this practice, the following overview will give you context on how the process works.

The Process of Body Scanning

Body scanning is a structured practice that systematically directs your attention to different areas of the body. Once you master the basic process, it usually takes less than fifteen minutes to complete.

If time does not allow for a full body scan, you can use an abbreviated version of this tool, which takes less than three minutes. This is considered a "check-in" and is described in the Techniques section below.

Elements of Body Scanning

1. Find a position that allows you to relax but remain alert. This could be lying down on a firm surface, sitting upright in a chair, or even standing. The key is to feel stable and at ease, with minimal distractions.

2. Before starting, set a clear intention for the practice. This might involve cultivating awareness, reducing tension, or simply observing the body as it is. Intentions help ground the practice and keep your focus steady.

3. Start by taking a few deep breaths, directing your attention to the sensation of the breath entering and leaving your body. Notice the way your chest rises and falls or the coolness of the air at the tip of your nose.

4. Choose whether to begin at the top of your head and work downward or start at your feet and work upward.

5. Bring your attention to one area of the body at a time. For example, you can start with your toes, feet, ankles, or legs. Observe the sensations in each area. This could be warmth, coolness, tingling, tension, or even a lack of sensation. The key is to simply notice the sensation(s).

6. If you encounter an area of tension, pain, or discomfort, pause and gently focus your attention there. Notice the qualities of the sensation(s) and explore how they change as you continue to observe. Avoid trying to "fix" anything; instead, approach sensations with curiosity and acceptance.

7. Once you've scanned the entire body, take a moment to rest, noticing how the body feels overall and any shifts in sensation, relaxation, or awareness.

 **TIPS**

Return to the breath if the mind wanders. It's natural for your mind to wander during body scanning. When this happens, gently bring your focus back to the body part you were observing or to the breath as a way to re-anchor your attention.

Gentle stretching during body scanning allows you to notice and respond to areas of tightness or discomfort. Stretching specific muscle groups while focusing on sensations encourages deeper engagement with the body.

Techniques for Body Scanning

Guided Visualization

Using self-guided or prewritten scripts, visualization can enhance body scanning by creating a narrative focus for attention. For example, imagining a wave of relaxation slowly moving through each part of the body can help anchor awareness and reduce wandering thoughts. Studies in cognitive behavioral techniques show that visualization can enhance relaxation and reduce stress by engaging the mind in structured, calming imagery.[5]

Somatic Touch or Pressure Techniques

Lightly applying pressure to specific areas of the body during scanning, such as pressing the palms into the thighs or placing a hand on the stomach, can enhance awareness of those areas. Research in somatic therapies shows that touch can improve the mind-body connection by engaging neural circuits associated with interoception (internal body awareness).[6]

Body Scanning Check-Ins

If you only have a few minutes to engage with body scanning, this technique is an effective way to utilize this tool in less than three minutes. You can also implement body scanning in real-time as illustrated in Ms. Taylor's vignette (below).

- Begin by pausing and directing your attention inward.

- Take a few slow, steady breaths and choose just a few anchor points to observe, such as your jaw, shoulders, chest, hands, or abdomen.

- Bring awareness to any sensations present in those areas: tightness, ease, warmth, pressure, or even numbness, and try to intentionally release the sensation while you focus on it. For example, if you notice your shoulders are raised and feel tight, drop your shoulders and release the tension.

Implementing Body Scanning

Ms. Taylor

Ms. Taylor, a special education teacher, used to push through the day without paying much attention to the tension building in her body. By the afternoon, she often felt drained, irritable, and less patient with her students. When she left for the

(Continued)

(Continued)

Key Considerations: Ms. Taylor

The above scenario illustrates how to integrate body scanning both in real-time and through dedicated practice. Ms. Taylor uses this tool proactively, setting aside time each day to check in with her body while also employing quick scans throughout the day to prevent stress from accumulating. This dual approach allows her to maintain greater self-awareness and remain attuned to subtle physical cues that might otherwise go unnoticed.

Ms. Taylor integrates guided visualization, a technique that actively shapes neural pathways responsible for emotional regulation and attentional control. By directing focused attention to her breath and pairing it with visualization techniques, she strengthens the brain's prefrontal cortex, which governs executive function and impulse control, while downregulating the amygdala, the brain's center for processing stress and threat responses.[7]

Over time, her brain becomes conditioned to recognize stress in its early stages and reset before it builds to a disruptive level.

Technological Options for Body Scanning

Insight Timer provides free, guided meditations specifically focused on body scans with options for different durations.

Smiling Mind offers a mindfulness app that includes structured programs for body scanning, especially for stress management.

Calm features guided body scan meditations in its mindfulness offerings, with a range of lengths and voices.

Muse is a biofeedback device and app pairing that supports body scan practices, tracking stress responses during meditation.

TRIPP (VR Platforms) offers immersive body scan practices within virtual environments, creating a focused and engaging experience.

Implementing Body Scanning With Technology

Mr. Johnson

Mr. Johnson is an assistant principal who supports the school's special education classroom. He spends much of his day juggling administrative tasks, addressing staff concerns, and responding to student crises. After a particularly difficult morning, including a tense meeting about IEP compliance, he feels both physically and mentally drained. The weight of the morning lingers in his body, settling as stiffness in his lower back and a dull ache in his shoulders. He recognizes that if he carries this tension into his next meeting, his ability to engage fully will be compromised.

Before his next commitment, he takes out his phone and opens the Smiling Mind app for an eight-minute guided body scan. Sitting in his office, he closes his eyes and listens as the narration leads him to focus on different areas of his body, beginning with the sensation of his feet against the floor and gradually moving upward. As he follows the instructions, he notices how his tension is not just emotional but physical, manifesting in a tightened jaw and the rigid way he is

(Continued)

(Continued)

Key Considerations: Mr. Johnson

Mr. Johnson experiences how body scanning can serve as a powerful tool for resetting his nervous system, preventing accumulated stress from dictating his interactions. By choosing a guided body scanning exercise through the Smiling Mind app, he strengthens his ability to recognize and release tension in real time, training his brain to recover more efficiently from high-pressure situations. Over time, this practice allows him to navigate the demands of his role with greater emotional agility, ensuring that each new challenge is met with presence rather than residual stress from the last.

MINDFULNESS

Tool Number Three: Mindfulness

Imagine walking into your classroom or office feeling overwhelmed before the day begins. Each stressor adds to those feelings, causing your emotions to intensify. Before you know it, you are reacting from a negative state of mind rather than intentionally responding. Mindfulness offers a way to break cycles like these.

Mindfulness is the practice of being fully present and aware of your thoughts, emotions, and bodily sensations without judgment. While its origins stem from ancient contemplative traditions, research today firmly establishes mindfulness as an evidence-based tool used to promote emotional balance and self-awareness. in educational settings.[8] Its benefits extend far beyond stress reduction, helping individuals develop a clearer understanding of their emotions and reactions.

In high-stress environments like special education, where teachers and administrators constantly balance student needs, regulatory requirements, and emotional demands, mindfulness provides a way to stay grounded and intentional. The goal of using this tool is to notice frustration (or other emotions) building before an impulsive reaction takes place. This awareness creates the opportunity for you to choose a targeted response instead of a quick reaction that might make matters worse.

Techniques for Mindfulness

Mindful Breathing

Focus on your breath, noticing each inhale and exhale. Pay attention to how it feels as the air moves through your nose or mouth and into your lungs. Try breathing in for four counts, pausing for two, and exhaling for six counts. If your mind wanders, gently bring it back to your breath without judgment. Research on breath awareness and vagus nerve activation shows that slow, intentional breathing activates the parasympathetic nervous system and lowers anxiety.[9]

Body Awareness Walks

Take a slow, deliberate walk, paying close attention to the feeling of your feet connecting with the ground, the rhythm of your steps, and the movement of your body. As you walk, bring awareness to internal sensations. Notice how your breathing changes, whether your shoulders are tense, or if any areas of your body feel constricted or relaxed. This practice combines movement-based mindfulness with interoception, both of which support stress reduction and nervous system regulation.

Mindful Observation

Choose an object (such as a pen or plant) and observe it closely, focusing on its texture, color, and shape without assigning meaning to the object. Notice details like shadows, reflections, or how light hits different surfaces. Observe any patterns, variations in color, or subtle changes as you continue looking. If your thoughts wander, gently redirect your focus back to what you are observing. This practice is based on focused attention meditation, which research shows enhances cognitive processing and attentional control.[10] It shifts the brain out of rumination and reactive thinking, making it a simple yet effective tool for professionals needing to reset their focus throughout the day.

Guided Scripts

Use prewritten mindfulness prompts to guide your practice. Prompts should encourage acceptance-based mindfulness. Take thirty seconds to sit quietly with each prompt before moving to the next one. Example prompts:

1. What emotions am I feeling right now, and where do I notice them in my body?

2. Instead of pushing discomfort away, how can I observe it with curiosity?

3. What is one small thing I can appreciate about this moment?

The above examples are meant to guide you in this practice. It is most helpful for you to create your own prompts, and it is not necessary to use more than one prompt if time does not allow it. This approach is particularly useful for those who experience stress but need to remain present for their students or colleagues.

Implementing Mindfulness

Ms. Reyes

Ms. Reyes, a school social worker, enters her office feeling irritated. The family she is about to meet will likely reject the resources needed for their child, as they have done in the past. Ms. Reyes feels strongly that the child must have new glasses and clothes that fit properly. Both are crucial to his self-esteem and success in school. However, the family has historically dismissed her suggestions or has become insulted when she offers help.

Recognizing her irritation and negative mindset, Ms. Reyes engages in her guided script before the family arrives. She asks herself two questions:

- What emotions am I feeling, and where are these feelings in my body?

- What are some small things I can appreciate about this moment and the meeting to follow?

Ms. Reyes labeled one feeling as "frustrated," and she felt it as tension in her jaw and tightness across her shoulders. She also noted feeling discouraged, which felt like a heavy weight in her chest. She took a moment to engage with her feelings, then shifted to the second prompt. Ms. Reyes felt appreciative that the family continues to show up for meetings, which allows her to advocate for the student and present solutions. She also felt grateful for the quiet moment to center herself and collect her thoughts before the meeting.

This short exercise helped Ms. Reyes shift her irritation and assumptions to a more grounded, open stance before entering the meeting. Although she cannot force the parents to accept the resources that would help their child, she has a better chance of helping them understand the importance of these supports when she approaches the conversation from a place of calm collaboration rather than frustrated advocacy.

Key Considerations: Ms. Reyes

Ms. Reyes experiences how mindfulness provides a way to reset her emotional state before entering a challenging interaction. By intentionally shifting her awareness to the present moment and acknowledging her feelings without judgment, she disrupts the cycle of automatic irritation and gives her brain the chance to approach the situation with greater clarity. Each time she engages in this practice, she strengthens the neural pathways that support attentional control and emotional regulation, reinforcing her ability to shift from reactive frustration to intentional collaboration more quickly.

Over time, this process rewires her brain's default response to challenging meetings in general. As a result, she can remain engaged and effective in difficult conversations and advocate for students with calm persistence.

Technological Options for Mindfulness

Headspace offers beginner-friendly mindfulness exercises, including short sessions on emotional awareness.

Calm features guided mindfulness practices for stress, anxiety, and emotional regulation, with customizable durations.

Insight Timer provides free mindfulness sessions, including themed options like "Mindfulness for Educators."

MyLife customizes mindfulness exercises based on how you feel in the moment, focusing on emotions and self-awareness.

FitMind combines mindfulness with neuroscience-based training, offering structured programs to develop emotional awareness.

Implementing Mindfulness With Technology

Mr. Nguyen

Mr. Nguyen, a principal managing a large school with a significant special education population, moves through his day at an exhausting pace, shifting from student concerns to staff needs to district expectations with little room to pause. By midday, he notices the weight of mental fatigue setting in. His patience

(Continued)

(Continued)

Key Considerations: Mr. Nguyen

Mr. Nguyen experiences how mindfulness strengthens his ability to engage with emotions rather than become consumed by them. By regularly stepping into a state of nonjudgmental awareness, he reinforces neural pathways that support emotional flexibility and cognitive clarity, making it easier to reset rather than carry stress from one moment to the next.[11] Over time, this practice rewires his brain's response to pressure, allowing him to remain focused and present even in high-stakes situations. As a result, he is better equipped to lead with composure, ensuring his decisions and interactions reflect intention rather than accumulated stress.

GRATITUDE PRACTICES

Tool Number Four: Gratitude Practices

What if a subtle shift in focus could transform your entire day? The practice of gratitude offers more than just a fleeting sense of appreciation. It has the power to reshape how you experience your work and your life. By deliberately noticing and valuing the small, meaningful moments, gratitude becomes a powerful antidote to stress and a catalyst for resilience.

Gratitude practices are not about generic positive thinking. They are intentional and reflective habits that cultivate a deeper sense of awareness and presence. This intentional focus provides a powerful counterbalance to the relentless pace and complexity of special education environments. Educators and administrators often find themselves managing emotionally charged situations, tight deadlines, and evolving challenges. Gratitude offers a practical and transformative approach to help you stay balanced amid the chaos.

Incorporating gratitude into daily routines not only shifts perspective; it also has a tangible impact on the brain. Research using functional MRI scans has shown that gratitude practices activate the prefrontal cortex, which is involved in emotional regulation and decision-making.[12] Regular gratitude practices increase neural sensitivity in pathways associated with feelings of reward and social bonding, and this may enhance your ability to handle stress and build resilience.[13]

When you recognize small victories, appreciate supportive colleagues, or acknowledge your own strengths, reward processing regions in your brain become more responsive. This shift promotes a positive mindset, which enhances and sustains your well-being.[14]

Techniques for Gratitude Practices

Gratitude Journaling

Write down three specific things you are grateful for each day. Focus on concrete moments, such as witnessing a student's progress or experiencing a colleague's support. Research on gratitude journaling indicates that this practice enhances emotional well-being, broadens an optimistic outlook, and fosters adaptive coping.[15]

Gratitude Letters

Write a heartfelt letter to someone who makes a meaningful difference in your life. Focus on specific moments, actions, or qualities that have touched you rather than general statements of appreciation. Instead of simply saying "I'm grateful for my friend Sarah," you might write "I'm grateful for how Sarah always remembers to check in on me after difficult days at work, and the way she listens without trying to fix everything."

The power of this technique lies in the details. Describe particular instances when a person's kindness, support, or presence mattered most to you. Explain how their actions affected you and why those moments were significant.

You can keep the letter private or send it. Either way, you will experience benefits. Gratitude letters shift your perspective toward gratitude and appreciation. This mental shift naturally counteracts stress and cultivates a more positive outlook.

Gratitude Reflection and Sharing

Set aside five minutes at the start or end of the day to reflect quietly on moments or people you are thankful for. Allow the feelings of gratitude to settle within you, creating a calming effect that helps regulate stress responses.

Incorporating gratitude practices into team meetings or classroom circles by inviting staff or students to share something they are grateful for is particularly effective. If you are a leader, you can ask your team members to write a short note of thanks to a staff member, highlighting something you appreciate or noticed about them. These simple practices not only foster a culture of positivity but also strengthen social bonds. Group gratitude practices have been linked to activating oxytocin-related pathways in the brain that facilitate trust and social cohesion.[16]

Implementing Gratitude Practices

Ms. Carter

Ms. Carter, a special education teacher, moves through her day balancing student needs, behavioral crises, and the administrative demands of IEP documentation and meetings. Today has been particularly difficult. One of her students refused to engage in his communication device trial, another eloped from the classroom, and the morning started with a tense parent discussion about behavioral interventions. As the final bell rings, she feels the weight of exhaustion pressing down, her mind already racing toward tomorrow's challenges.

Instead of carrying this stress home, Ms. Carter reaches for her Gratitude Notebook. She takes a deep breath and writes down three moments of gratitude: A student used his communication device without a prompt for the first time, her teaching assistant stepped in seamlessly to de-escalate a crisis, and a colleague left a supportive note on her desk. While writing, she feels a shift in her emotions. Instead of focusing exclusively on the day's struggles, she now lingers on its moments of connection and progress.

Ms. Carter finds that at the end of every day, no matter how challenging, she can always find positive moments. The more she engages in this practice, the more she notices these moments in real-time.

Key Considerations: Ms. Carter

Ms. Carter's experience shows how a simple, consistent gratitude practice can reshape an educator's emotional landscape. By deliberately shifting her attention to moments of progress and appreciation, she strengthens neural pathways associated with cognitive reappraisal and stress resilience.

Over time, this practice has rewired the way Ms. Carter processes stress. Each time she consciously focuses on positive moments, she reinforces her brain's ability to counterbalance the natural negativity bias that can lead to burnout.[17] This shift is critical for education teachers, who experience higher levels of emotional exhaustion and intensity in their roles.

Technological Options for Gratitude Practices

Grateful is a Gratitude Journal (iOS, Android): A digital gratitude journal for quickly recording daily moments of appreciation with optional prompts to guide reflection.

Presently provides a simple and free app for recording gratitude entries, featuring a minimalist design to keep focus on reflection.

Three Good Things prompts users to log three positive experiences each day, reinforcing the practice of noticing gratitude-worthy moments.

Reflectly combines journaling with gratitude prompts, offering AI-guided questions to encourage deeper reflection.

365 Gratitude adds gamification elements, encouraging users to reflect daily and earn rewards for maintaining their gratitude practice.

Insight Timer offers guided gratitude meditations to help users integrate mindful appreciation into their daily routines.

Implementing Gratitude Practices With Technology

Dr. Lee

Dr. Lee, a special education compliance administrator, oversees a large school district. She spends her day balancing administrative demands, staff needs, and the complex challenges of supporting special education services. Today, a disciplinary

(Continued)

(Continued)

Key Considerations: Dr. Lee

Dr. Lee's experience underscores how intentional gratitude practices help school leaders manage the emotional toll of overseeing special education services. Leaders frequently navigate high-stakes decision-making related to IEP compliance, crisis intervention, and staff burnout. By engaging in daily gratitude reflection, Dr. Lee strengthens neural circuits associated with stress reduction and cognitive reappraisal, allowing her to approach these challenges with a more measured and constructive mindset.

When school leaders cultivate personal resilience, they model emotional steadiness for their staff, creating an environment where special educators feel supported in their emotionally demanding roles. Over time, Dr. Lee's practice of gratitude doesn't just benefit her. It reinforces a culture of appreciation, motivation, and collective growth in both general and special education settings.

EXPRESSIVE WRITING

Tool Number Five: Expressive Writing

The challenges of special educators do not arrive one at a time. They cascade throughout the day, building layers of stress without natural breaks for recovery. Difficult conversations about student placements, behavioral crises that disrupt carefully planned schedules, frustrated parents who need immediate answers, and staff shortages pile additional responsibilities onto already overflowing workloads.

Without opportunities to reset between crises, the emotional toll accumulates, following you home in the evening and greeting you again the next morning, creating a cycle where yesterday's stress becomes today's starting point.

What if instead of carrying this tension home with you, you pull out a notebook, set a timer for ten minutes, and just start writing without thinking or judging? You write about the frustration, the disappointment, and maybe the self-doubt. When the timer goes off, you stop and feel a wave of release. That is the power of expressive writing.

This tool focuses on processing deeply personal or emotional topics, particularly those related to stress and unaddressed feelings. Unlike reflective journaling, which emphasizes analysis and learning, expressive writing is centered on emotional release and catharsis. The practice involves writing continuously about specific emotional experiences without concern for grammar or structure. It typically begins with selecting a moment or emotion to explore, setting a time limit (often ten to twenty minutes), and writing without editing or filtering thoughts. Afterward, individuals may choose to reflect on their writing or simply let it stand as an emotional release.

Long-term benefits of expressive writing are well-documented. Studies show that regular practice can lead to improved emotional regulation, lower stress levels, and increased resilience in high-pressure environments.[18] For professionals who must maintain composure and clarity in their roles, expressive writing provides a safe and private method for processing difficult emotions. By translating raw emotions into words, the brain engages in a form of cognitive processing that transforms the emotional experience, making it more manageable and less overwhelming.[19]

For educators and leaders, this tool is not just a way to manage stress but a proactive strategy to build a sustainable approach to emotional well-being. By incorporating expressive writing into their routines, professionals can develop a habit of self-regulation that enhances their ability to support students, colleagues, and themselves.

Techniques for Expressive Writing

Freewriting

Freewriting involves setting a timer from five to fifteen minutes and writing continuously without pausing to edit, analyze, or structure thoughts. The focus is on allowing raw emotions to emerge without interruption. This method is useful for processing complex emotions that may feel overwhelming when spoken aloud. The key is to keep the pen moving or fingers typing, even if thoughts become disorganized. Freewriting helps individuals bypass mental barriers, providing an uninhibited space to release frustration, sadness, or anxiety.

Stream-of-Consciousness Writing

Stream-of-consciousness writing allows thoughts to flow freely onto the page without restriction or direction. It is best to allow five to fifteen minutes, depending on how much time you have available. Unlike freewriting, which may focus on a particular event or emotion, this method follows wherever the mind naturally goes. The goal is to bypass conscious filtering and uncover deeper thoughts or emotions. Writing in this way often reveals unexpected insights and patterns, making it useful for exploring subconscious feelings and emotional undercurrents that may not surface in structured writing.

Prompt-Based Expressive Writing

This method involves responding to specific prompts designed to evoke emotional exploration. It is customary to spend three to five minutes per prompt. Prompts might include questions like, *What is weighing on me today?* or *When was the last time I felt truly at peace? What would I tell a colleague who was having my exact same day?* or *What am I struggling to understand today?* Using prompts can help guide the writing process, particularly when emotions feel too scattered or when it is difficult to identify the root of the distress. However, it is important to keep your responses to the prompt(s) unstructured and free-flowing.

Research suggests that using structured prompts can facilitate deeper emotional processing and enhance self-awareness.[20]

Transition Writing

This brief technique is well-suited if you need to process emotions quickly between activities. Set aside just three to five minutes to write rapidly and without editing about whatever you're feeling in the moment. There should be no structure or judgement, statements may be something like, "I am so frustrated right now I could scream. That meeting was a disaster, and I feel like I failed that kid. My head is pounding, and I just want to go home and forget this whole day happened." The goal is to release the emotional weight onto paper so you can leave it behind rather than carrying it with you.

Implementing Expressive Writing

Ms. Williams

Ms. Williams, a school social worker, spends her days supporting students, teachers, and families through complex emotional and behavioral challenges. Today was particularly difficult. A heated conversation with a parent left her feeling drained and frustrated. The parent, overwhelmed and defensive, questioned every intervention Ms. Williams suggested, making it clear that she did not trust the school's approach. Though she remained professional, the emotional weight of the exchange lingers as Ms. Williams prepares to head home.

Before leaving, she sits down with her journal, sets a timer to alarm at ten minutes, and writes freely, without filtering her words or trying to craft a solution. She allows her frustration onto the page, acknowledging her feelings without judgment. As she writes, she begins to feel her body relax. The tightness in her chest eases, and the residual frustration that had threatened to follow her home begins to dissipate.

When the timer goes off, Ms. Williams feels a sense of release and clarity that allows her to end her day from a place of balance and composure.

Key Considerations: Ms. Williams

Ms. Williams' experience demonstrates how expressive writing creates a powerful neurological shift, offering more than just an outlet for emotions. Translating feelings into words engages the prefrontal cortex, the area of the brain responsible for cognitive processing, reflection, and emotional regulation.[21] This shift to higher-order thinking promotes a state of calm and allows for greater perspective.

Consistent expressive writing reinforces neural pathways that support resilience, helping individuals respond to stress with greater clarity and stability.[22] Over time, this practice not only reduces immediate stress but also enhances the brain's ability to regulate emotions more effectively.

Technological Options for Expressive Writing

Expressive writing requires a completely free and uninterrupted flow of thoughts and emotions, making traditional tools like a blank document on a desktop or laptop the best technology options. Unlike other self-awareness practices that benefit from apps offering prompts, structure, or guided reflection, expressive writing thrives in an unstructured space, where thoughts can emerge naturally without external influence. Using apps or platforms with built-in prompts, reminders can disrupt the free-flow process by introducing external cues or encouraging analysis and reflection too early. These interruptions can shift the focus away from authentic emotional release and toward structured thinking, and this diminishes the therapeutic effect of expressive writing. Instead, basic word processing tools like Microsoft Word, Google Docs, and Apple Notes provide the open and unstructured space necessary for effective expressive writing.

AFFECT LABELING

Tool Number Six: Affect Labeling

Imagine having the power to shift your stress response in an instant. That's exactly what affect labeling does. It is a straightforward yet transformative tool for building self-awareness by naming emotions as they arise. Often described as "putting feelings into words," affect labeling creates a bridge between raw emotion and clear thinking, allowing you to regain control in real-time.

When you label your emotions, something remarkable happens: The intensity of those emotions decreases, and a sense of clarity takes hold.[23] Instead of being swept away by a rush of frustration or overwhelm, you become grounded, more aware of what you are feeling and why. For example, if a teacher having a moment of high stress pauses and says to herself, "I'm feeling overwhelmed and frustrated," she activates the thinking part of her brain, shifting from a reactive fight-or-flight state to a more thoughtful, measured response.

This tool isn't just about managing stress. It's about transforming it.

Techniques for Affect Labeling

Internal Identification

Pause when you experience heightened emotions and silently name what you are feeling. By acknowledging specific emotions (e.g., "I feel irritated"), you create space between the emotion and your reaction, promoting a more thoughtful response in the moment.

Visual Emotion Charts

Use tools like a feelings wheel to identify specific emotions and gauge their intensity (see Figure 5.2). This visual approach not only helps pinpoint complex emotions but also encourages deeper self-awareness. Studies suggest that using emotion charts enhances emotional intelligence by providing a structured method to explore and understand feelings.[24]

FIGURE 5.2 Feelings Wheel Example

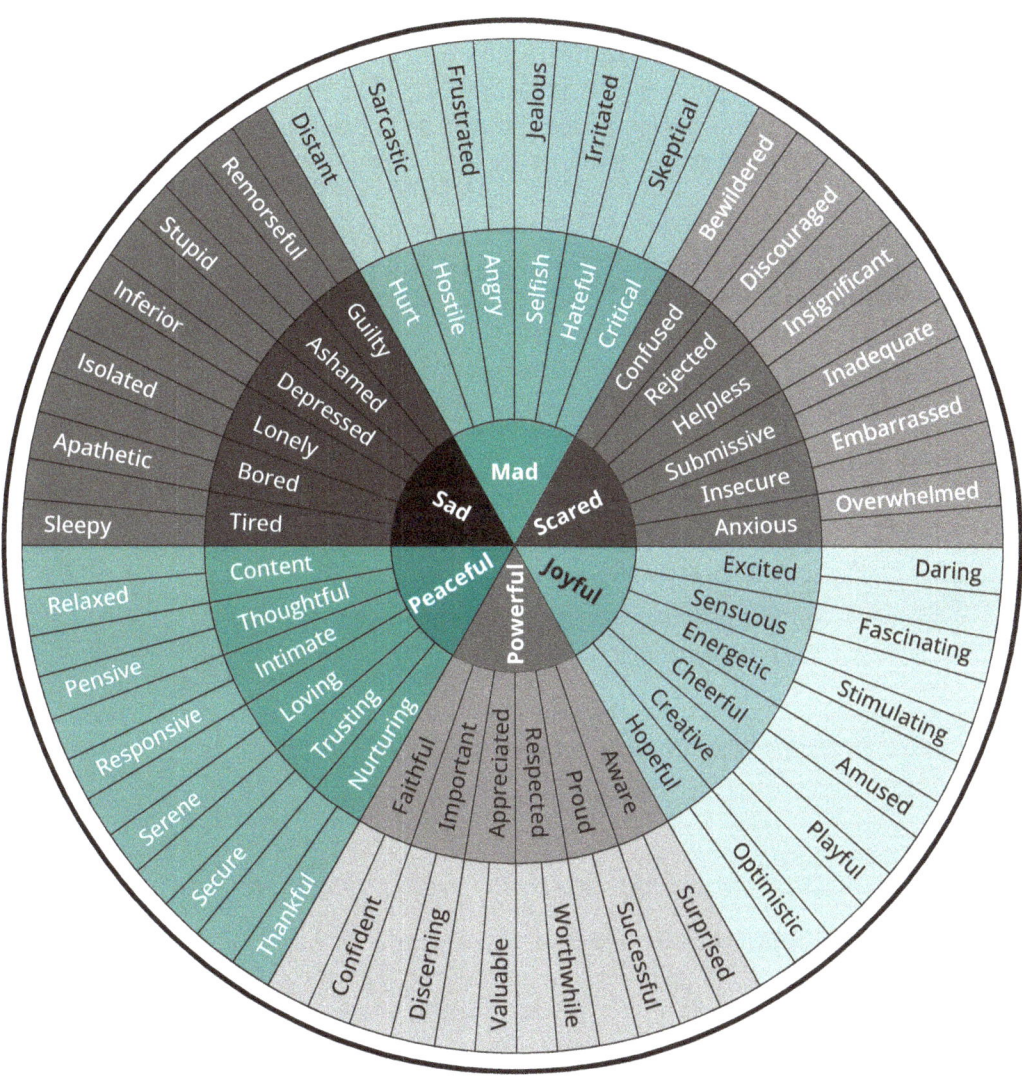

SOURCE: Wilcox, G. (1982). "The Feeling Wheel: A Tool for Expanding Awareness of Emotions and Increasing Spontaneity and Intimacy," *International Transactional Analysis Association*, reprinted by permission of Informa UK Limited, trading as Taylor & Francis Group, www.tandfonline.com on behalf of International Transactional Analysis Association.

Implementing Affect Labeling

Mr. Smith

Mr. Smith, a behavior specialist at an elementary school, stepped out of a classroom after assisting with a student who had a disruptive outburst during a math lesson. Though the student was now calm and the situation under control, Mr. Smith felt a surge of residual stress. His heart was still racing, and he noticed tightness in his jaw. He felt unsettled but couldn't pinpoint why.

Before walking into his next meeting, he pulls out the emotion wheel from his clipboard and scans it quietly in the hallway. As he focuses on the categories and specific words, he identifies "irritated," which connects to the core emotion of anger. Naming this emotion helps him recognize what drives his physical tension. He is angry because he suspects the classroom staff isn't consistently implementing the student's Behavior Intervention Plan (BIP), and that is what caused the outburst.

This self-awareness interrupts his assumptions, allowing him to consider that the classroom staff may be implementing the BIP regularly, but it may need revising, or perhaps the staff members are not clear on how to use it. Instead of reacting from frustration and assumptions, he schedules time to observe the classroom later in the week to gather data on the plan and its implementation.

By identifying his emotions, Mr. Smith creates enough space to settle his thoughts and refocus. Within minutes, he feels more composed and ready to continue his day with clarity rather than carrying unresolved tension into his next interaction.

Key Considerations: Mr. Smith

When Mr. Smith uses the emotion chart to label what he is feeling, his brain shifts from reactive to reflective processing. This process allows for greater emotional clarity and shortens the duration of physiological stress.

Technological Options for Affect Labeling

Moodnotes is a journaling app that helps users label their emotions and understand triggers while offering suggestions for reframing negative thoughts.

Daylio includes a mood tracker that allows users to label emotions throughout the day and visualize patterns in their emotional experiences.

Youper provides an AI-powered app that guides users through conversations about their emotions, helping them identify and name what they are feeling.

Insight Timer offers guided meditations and exercises focused on affect labeling and emotional awareness.

Mood Meter is based on research by the Yale Center for Emotional Intelligence; this app helps users identify and label emotions while learning about their underlying causes.

Implementing Affect Labeling With Technology

Dr. Patel

Dr. Patel, an assistant principal overseeing the school's special education program, experiences emotional shifts throughout the day. Her morning began with an uplifting classroom visit, where she observed a student with a speech delay confidently participating in a small-group discussion. Then by lunchtime, she found herself discouraged after a difficult conversation with a teacher, feeling overwhelmed by student behavior challenges. As she steps into her office for a brief afternoon break, she recognizes the emotional tug-of-war pulling her in different directions.

To stay grounded, Dr. Patel opens the Moodnotes app, a practice she has integrated into her routine. The app prompts her to describe how she feels, offering a spectrum of emotional words to choose from. She selects "stressed" and "discouraged" and writes a short note about the earlier conflict. The app suggests reframing her perspective, reminding her that her stress is tied to a single moment rather than defining her leadership as a whole. As she considers this, she feels her frustration loosen, replaced by a clearer sense of perspective.

For school leaders, this skill is critical. Without awareness and processing, emotional residue from one interaction can unintentionally shape the next. By consistently practicing affect labeling, Dr. Patel strengthens neural pathways that allow her to approach each challenge with fresh clarity rather than accumulated frustration.

Key Considerations: Dr. Patel

Dr. Patel's experience highlights the importance of emotional regulation in special education leadership. Administrators overseeing special education programs must navigate emotionally charged conversations daily, whether addressing teacher burnout, handling IEP disputes, or supporting students with complex needs. Without intentional affect labeling, stress can build unchecked, affecting decision-making and leadership presence.

By using an app to support this practice, Dr. Patel reinforces a habit of reflection and cognitive reappraisal. Over time, she trains her brain to respond to challenges with greater emotional flexibility, ensuring that she remains composed and focused even in high-pressure situations. This ability not only benefits her resilience but also strengthens the culture of emotional intelligence within her school, fostering an environment where educators and students alike feel supported in managing their emotions.

CHAPTER SUMMARY

Chapter Five provides six evidence-based tools designed to cultivate self-awareness among special educators, leaders, and professionals. These tools include reflective journaling, body scanning, mindfulness, gratitude practices, affect labeling, and expressive writing. Each tool offers a distinct approach to understanding and managing emotions, thoughts, and behaviors in demanding professional environments. The tools and techniques presented are summarized in Table 5.1.

TABLE 5.1 Self-Awareness Tools and Techniques

TOOL	DESCRIPTION	TECHNIQUES
Reflective Journaling	Reflective writing allows you to recognize and understand emotional patterns and triggers, which gives you the power to make intentional adjustments that serve your well-being.	Select Columns Scenarios Cause-and-Effect Sketch Color Coding
Body Scanning	Body scanning is a guided practice that involves mentally scanning the body to notice tension, discomfort, or other sensations linked to emotions so that you can handle stress before it escalates.	Mindful Stretching Breath Integration Guided Visualization Somatic Touch Meditative Walking

TOOL	DESCRIPTION	TECHNIQUES
Mindfulness	Practices that involve focusing attention on the present moment to develop clearer understanding of emotions in a way that helps you stay grounded and intentional.	Mindful Breathing Body Awareness Walks Mindful Observation Compassion-Based Mindfulness Guided Scripts Mindful Observation
Gratitude Practices	Reflecting on positive aspects of life helps shift attention from reactive states to constructive emotions, enhancing self-awareness of one's emotional baseline.	Gratitude Journaling Gratitude Letters Gratitude Reflection Gratitude Sharing
Expressive Writing	Writing without judgement helps process and release deeper emotions resulting in a sense of release and calm.	Freewriting Gratitude-Infused Writing Stream-of-Consciousness Prompt-Based Narrative Writing
Affect Labeling	The process of naming emotions brings an immediate shift from reactive emotions to conscious consideration.	Internal Identification Visual Emotion Charts Verbal Expression

Reflective journaling encourages you to document your daily experiences and emotional responses, helping you to identify patterns and gain deeper insights into behavior. Body scanning involves a mindfulness technique that focuses on physical sensations, allowing you to recognize stress and tension before they escalate. Mindfulness practices, including breathing exercises and guided observation, promote present-moment awareness, helpsing to reduce reactive behaviors, while gratitude practices focus on positive experiences, building resilience and reinforcing a sense of well-being. Expressive writing gives you a private outlet for processing emotions, particularly in high-stress situations, by translating feelings into words, releasing your emotional tension. Finally, affect labeling provides a strategy for naming emotions as they arise, reducing their intensity, and supporting thoughtful responses.

NOTES

1. Bucknell, K. J., Kangas, M., Karin, E., & Crane, M. F. (2024). A randomized controlled trial comparing the effects of self-reflective writing focused on successful and unsuccessful coping experiences on resilience. *Stress and Health, 40*(2), e3311. doi: 10.1002/smi.3311

2. Thoele, D. G., Gunalp, C., Baran, D., Harris, J., Moss, D., Donovan, R., Li, Y., & Getz, M. A. (2020). Health care practitioners and families writing together: The three-minute mental makeover. *The Permanente Journal, 24,* 19.056. doi: 10.7812/TPP/19.056

3. Yadav, S. (2022, July). Reflective journals: A tool for self-reflection, self-awareness and professional development. *Educational Resurgence Journal.* https://www.researchgate.net/publication/372350059_Reflective_Journals_A_tool_for_Self-Reflection_Self-Awareness_and_Professional_Development

4. Damasio, A. R. (2010). *Self Comes to mind: Constructing the conscious brain.* Pantheon.

5. Reiss, N., Warnecke, I., Tolgou, T., Krampen, D., Luka-Krausgrill, U., & Rohrmann, S. (2017). Effects of cognitive behavioral therapy with relaxation versus imagery rescripting on test anxiety: A randomized controlled trial. *Journal of Affective Disorders, 208,* 483–489. 10.1016/j.jad.2016.10.039

6. Casals-Gutiérrez, S., & Abbey, H. (2020). Interoception, mindfulness and touch: A meta-review of functional MRI studies. International *Journal of Osteopathic Medicine, 35,* 22–23. https://www.journalofosteopathicmedicine.com/article/S1746-0689(18)30158-5/abstract

7. Tang, Y. Y., Hölzel, B. K., & Posner, M. I. (2015). The neuroscience of mindfulness meditation. *Nature Reviews Neuroscience, 16*(4), 213–225. doi: 10.1038/nrn3916

8. Jiménez-Picón, N., Romero-Martín, M., Ponce-Blandón, J. A., Ramirez-Baena, L., Palomo-Lara, J. C., & Gómez-Salgado, J. The relationship between mindfulness and emotional intelligence as a protective factor for healthcare professionals: Systematic review. *International Journal of Environmental Research and Public Health, 18*(10), 5491. DOI: 10.3390/ijerph18105491

9. Magnon, V., Dutheil, F., & Vallet, G. T. (2021). Benefits from one session of deep and slow breathing on vagal tone and anxiety in young and older adults. *Scientific Reports 11,* 19267. https://doi.org/10.1038/s41598-021-98736-9

10. Tang, Y. Y., Posner, M. I., Yan, R. X., Ma, Y. H., Wang, J. H., Feng, S. G., Yu, Q. B., Sui, D. N., Rothbart, M. K., & Fan, M. (2007). Short-term meditation training improves attention and self-regulation. *Proceedings of the National Academy of Sciences, 104*(43), 17152–56. https://doi.org/10.1073/pnas.0707678104 (2007).

11. Lutz, A., Dunne, J. D., & Davidson, R. J. (2007). Meditation and the neuroscience of consciousness. In P. D. Zelazo, M. Moscovitch, & E. Thompson. (Eds.). *The Cambridge Handbook of Consciousness* (pp. 499–554). Cambridge University Press.

12. Fox, G. R., Kaplan, B., Damasio, A., & Damasio, H. (2015). Neural correlates of gratitude: An fMRI study. *Frontiers in Psychology, 6,* 1491. doi.org/10.3389/fpsyg.2015.01491

13. Karns, C. M., Moore, W. D., & Mayr, U. (2017). The cultivation of gratitude: a functional MRI study of change with gratitude practice. *Frontiers in Human Neuroscience, 11*, 599. https://doi.org/10.3389/fnhum.2017.00599

14. Prathik, K., Wong, J., McInnis, S., Gabana, N., & W. Brown, J. W. (2016). The effects of gratitude expression on neural activity. *NeuroImage, 128*, 1–10. https://doi.org/10.1016/j.neuroimage.2015.12.040Get rights and content

15. Emmons, R. A., & McCullough, M. E. (2003). Counting blessings versus burdens: An experimental investigation of gratitude and subjective well-being in daily life. *Journal of Personality and Social Psychology, 84*(2) (2003): 377–89. doi: 10.1037//0022-3514.84.2.377

16. Algoe, Sara B., & Way, B. M. Evidence for a role of the oxytocin system, indexed by genetic variation in CD38, in the social bonding effects of expressed gratitude. *Social Cognitive and Affective Neuroscience, 9*(12), 1855–61. https://pubmed.ncbi.nlm.nih.gov/24396004/

17. Kiken, L. G., & Shook, N. J. (2011). Looking Up: Mindfulness increases positive judgments and reduces negativity bias. *Social Psychological and Personality Science, 2*(4), 425–431. https://doi.org/10.1177/1948550610396585

18. Pennebaker, J. W., & Smyth, J. M. (2016). *Opening up by writing it down: How expressive writing improves health and eases emotional pain* (3rd ed.). Guilford Press.

19. Baikie, K. A., & Wilhelm, K. Emotional and physical health benefits of expressive writing. (2005). *Advances in Psychiatric Treatment, 11*(5), 338–346. doi: https://doi.org/10.1192/apt.11.5.338

20. Sloan, D. M., & Marx, B. P. (2004). Taking Pen to Hand: Evaluating Theories Underlying the Written Disclosure Paradigm. *Clinical Psychology: Science and Practice, 11*(2), 121–137. doi:10.1093/clipsy.bph062

21. Lieberman, M. D., Eisenberger, N. I., Crockett, M. J., Tom, S. M., Pfeifer, J. H., & Way, B. M. (2007). Putting feelings into words: Affect labeling disrupts amygdala activity in response to affective stimuli. *Psychological Science, 18*(5), 421–428. https://doi.org/10.1111/j.1467-9280.2007.01916.x

22. Guo, L. T. (2023). The delayed, durable effect of expressive writing on depression, anxiety, and stress: a meta-analytic review of studies with long-term follow-ups. *British Journal of Clinical Psychology, 62*(1), 272–297. https://doi.org/10.1111/bjc.12408

23. Lieberman, M. D., Eisenberger, N. I., Crockett, M. J., Tom, S. M., Pfeifer, J. H., & Way, B. M. (2007). Putting feelings into words: Affect labeling disrupts amygdala activity in response to affective stimuli. *Psychological Science, 18*(5), 421–428. https://doi.org/10.1111/j.1467-9280.2007.01916.x

24. Brackett, M. A., & Rivers, S. E. Transforming students' lives with social and emotional learning. In J. A. Durlak, C. E. Domitrovich, R. P. Weissberg, & T. P. Gullotta (Eds). *Handbook of social and emotional learning: Research and practice.* (2015). Guilford Press, 497–513.

CHAPTER 6

Developing Self-Regulation

Imagine a fire drill just ended and students are flooding back into your classroom. The energy is high and frantic; students are scattered throughout the room, and your attempts to bring order disappear into the chaos. In moments like these, self-regulation becomes more than just a concept. It becomes an immediate, practical strategy to help you regain control and take effective action.

Where self-*awareness* shines a light on your emotions, self-*regulation* guides your emotions toward intentional responses, bridging the gap between awareness and action. For professionals working in high-pressure environments like special education, self-regulation is a skill that truly makes all the difference in becoming the best that you can be.[1]

WHAT SELF-REGULATION TOOLS DO

When you encounter a significant stressor, the brain reacts almost instantly. Its first priority is survival.[2] Without conscious thought, the brain shifts into high alert and prepares to respond by activating the amygdala (which governs fear and threat detection) and overriding the prefrontal cortex (the part of the brain responsible for reasoning).[3] This kind of response serves you well if you are in real danger. In a professional setting, however, fear-based reactions can cloud judgment, damage relationships, and lead to poor decisions.

Deliberate efforts to self-regulate make it possible to interrupt the automatic stress response. Self-regulation allows you to regain clarity and access your higher reasoning abilities, giving you the power to *respond* instead of *react*. This allows you to lead with purpose, even under pressure.

Consider the example in the opening paragraph of this chapter. A *reactive* response might be to clap your hands loudly and raise your voice while instructing everyone to sit down and be quiet. This response ensures that your emotional tension remains high, and while some students may comply, others are likely to become louder, matching the volume and intensity of your voice.

A *responsive* approach might begin with a pause amid the chaos to use a self-regulation tool like box breathing (described in the next chapter). After three cycles of breathing in for four counts, holding for four counts, exhaling for four counts, and holding again for four counts, your stress levels decrease, and you begin to process the situation more clearly. From a position of composure and clarity, you may choose the following strategy: Move to a position in the room that allows you to assess and select which students are the most escalated. Keeping your tone steady and firm, intentionally approach the most escalated students, make eye contact, and provide clear, specific directions as you guide each student to their seat. A logical result of this approach is that noise and activity levels naturally decrease because the most disruptive students are now calm and seated. This allows you to remain composed and direct the rest of the class without raising your voice. By using breathwork as a self-regulation tool, you interrupt the automatic stress response and engage your ability to think and form a plan of action.

WHY SELF-REGULATION TOOLS WORK

Self-regulation tools build upon the foundation of self-awareness by using emotional insight to guide actions. The previous chapters highlighted how identifying and labeling emotions shifts brain activity from the reactive amygdala to the more thoughtful prefrontal cortex. Self-regulation goes a step further and strengthens the brain's ability to override automatic responses. While both self-awareness and self-regulation engage the prefrontal cortex, they activate different regions. Self-awareness primarily involves the *medial* prefrontal cortex, which processes and contextualizes emotions.[4] In contrast, self-regulation engages the *dorsolateral* prefrontal cortex to enhance cognitive control and the *anterior cingulate* cortex to mediate conflicts between impulse and intention.[5] This deeper engagement enables the brain to transition from reactive states to thoughtful, goal-directed responses.[6]

The physiological benefits of self-regulation are equally important. Research indicates that self-regulation practices like controlled breathing and grounding not only reduce cortisol levels but also activate the parasympathetic nervous system, promoting a state of calm.[7] These physiological changes improve focus and decision-making under pressure, and this reinforces the habit of responding with intention.

Cognitive studies also support the idea that self-regulation strengthens neural pathways that support resilience.[8] With regular practice, the brain forms stronger connections that make composure and adaptability more automatic. Over time, this practice leads to a natural shift where thoughtful responses become second nature, reducing the likelihood of reactive behaviors in stressful scenarios.

QUICK SUMMARY

The more you practice self-regulation, the more it reshapes how you think, respond, and lead. Developing this skill strengthens your brain's ability to override impulses while reinforcing patterns of focus and intention. This changes the way you experience stress and pressure because you learn to effectively navigate intense situations, transforming the way you engage with students, colleagues, and stakeholders.

The self-regulation tools and techniques offered in the next chapter will give you the strategies you need to create environments where clarity and stability replace tension and reactivity.

Reflections

In the classroom example, the reactive teacher clapped loudly and raised her voice, escalating the chaos. The responsive teacher paused, used breathing to regain composure, then calmly approached the most escalated students with clear directions. Think of a recent challenging moment in your work:

1. Did you react automatically like the first teacher, or did you pause and respond intentionally like the second?

   _____

   _____

   _____

   _____

   _____

   _____

(Continued)

(Continued)

2.

3.

4.

NOTES

1. Brackett, M. A., Rivers, S. E., & Salovey, P. Emotional intelligence: Implications for personal, social, academic, and workplace success. (2011). *Social and Personality Psychology Compass 5*(1), 88–103. doi:10.1111/j.1751-9004.2010.00334.x

2. LeDoux, J. D. (1996). *The emotional brain: The mysterious underpinnings of emotional life*. Simon & Schuster.

3. Damasio, A. (1994). *Descartes' error: Emotion, reason, and the human brain*. Putnam.

4. Mitchell, J. P., Banaji, M. R., & Macrae, C. N. (2005). The link between social cognition and self-referential thought in the medial prefrontal cortex. *Journal of Cognitive Neuroscience, 17*(8), 1306–1315. doi: 10.1162/0898929055002418

5. Stuss, D. T., & Alexander, M. P. Executive functions and the frontal lobes: A conceptual view, (2000). *Psychological Research, 63*(3–4), 289–298. doi: 10.1007/s004269900007

6. Phan, K. L., Fitzgerald, D. A., Nathan, P. J., Moore, G. J., Uhde, T. W., & Tancer, M. E. (2005). Neural substrates for voluntary suppression of negative affect: A functional magnetic resonance imaging study. *Biological Psychiatry, 57*(3), 210–219. doi: 10.1016/j.biopsych.2004.10.030

7. Zaccaro, A., Piarulli, A., Laurino, M., Garbella, E., Menicucci, D., Neri, B., & Gemignani, A. (2018). How breath-control can change your life: A systematic review on psycho-physiological correlates of slow breathing. *Frontiers in Human Neuroscience, 12*, 353. https://doi.org/10.3389/fnhum.2018.00353

8. Tabibnia, G. (2020). An affective neuroscience model of boosting resilience in adults. *Neuroscience & Biobehavioral Reviews, 115*, 321–350. https://doi.org/10.1016/j.neubiorev.2020.05.00

CHAPTER 7

Self-Regulation Tools

Special educators regularly face intense, demanding situations that test their resilience. Whether dealing with a student in crisis, a litigious IEP meeting, or a frustrated parent, self-regulation skills are the key to navigating professional challenges with composure and confidence. We will explore five powerful tools that build or strengthen self-regulation: breathwork, cognitive reframing, grounding, progressive muscle relaxation, and DBT-informed strategies, each outlined in Figure 7.1. These tools and techniques offer you effective ways to manage stress, enhance focus, and foster a sense of calm. Whether you are looking for quick strategies to reset in the moment or long-term practices to support your overall well-being, the following options deliver results.

There is no shortage of methods designed to develop emotional regulation, but some are more practical and effective than others. The tools in this chapter were selected for their ability to give you meaningful results in real-world situations, and they are highly supported by research.

BREATHWORK

Tool Number One: Breathwork

When was the last time you truly noticed your breath? In the rush of everyday life, breathing is an unconscious rhythm in the background. Yet, with intention, you can transform it into a powerful tool for calm and clarity. Breathwork goes far beyond passive breathing. It offers a deliberate practice that taps into your nervous system, creating emotional balance and mental focus. These benefits are particularly valuable in high-pressure roles, common in special education.

Breathwork relies on *conscious* breathing techniques. Rather than breathing on autopilot, you intentionally direct each inhale and exhale, which

FIGURE 7.1   Selected Self-Regulation Tools

SELECTED TOOLS FOR SELF-REGULATION

Breathwork

Breathwork includes a variety of techniques that help you to breathe intentionally, promoting balance and composure quickly. This lowers stress and enhances focus in the moment.

Cognitive Reframing

Cognitive reframing identifies your negative thoughts, checking them for accuracy, and allows you to intentionally replace them with alternative perspectives.

Grounding

Grounding directs your attention to external stimuli to interrupt distressing emotions. It assists with regaining emotional balance, and anchoring you into the present moment.

PMR

Progressive Muscle Relaxation engages the body so that you can consciously release stress. Different muscle groups are systematically tensed and released, alleviating stress and promoting deep relaxation.

DBT-Informed Strategies

Dialectic Behavior Strategies help you disrupt reactivity in real time, when your nervous system is highly activated. This calms your body's stress response, allowing executive functioning to reengage

results in greater balance in both body and mind. In most breathwork practices, you begin by choosing a technique such as diaphragmatic breathing, box breathing, or paced breathing, then focus on slow, measured breaths for a few minutes. You can also add visualization or counting to enhance relaxation.

By controlling the rhythm and depth of your breath, you stimulate the parasympathetic nervous system, which is responsible for slowing heart rate, aiding digestion, and returning the body to a calmer state. This activation helps reduce cortisol levels, improve focus, and increase resilience, making it easier to stay composed and effective in challenging situations.[1]

Techniques for Breathwork

Diaphragmatic Breathing (Belly Breathing)

Diaphragmatic breathing, often called belly breathing, is a foundational breathwork technique that emphasizes full, deep breaths to engage the diaphragm. Unlike shallow chest breathing (which can trigger a stress response), diaphragmatic breathing encourages a state of relaxation by activating the parasympathetic nervous system. This practice not only helps lower your heart rate and blood pressure but also improves oxygen exchange, enhancing overall physical and mental well-being.[2]

To practice diaphragmatic breathing, begin by sitting or lying down in a comfortable position. Place one hand on your chest and the other on your abdomen to help monitor your breath. Inhale deeply through your nose, allowing your belly to expand as the diaphragm pulls air into the lungs. The hand on your abdomen should rise while the hand on your chest remains still. Exhale slowly and completely through your mouth, gently contracting your abdominal muscles to expel as much air as possible. Repeating this process for several minutes creates a sense of calm and reduces physical tension.

Box Breathing (Four-Square Breathing)

Box breathing, also known as four-square breathing, is a powerful technique often used by military personnel, first responders, and high-performance professionals to maintain focus and composure under pressure.[3] This method involves a simple, rhythmic breathing pattern: inhaling for four counts, holding the breath for four counts, exhaling for four counts, and holding again for four counts. The cycle is repeated several times, creating a balanced and steady breathing rhythm that calms both your mind and body.

The structured nature of box breathing helps regulate the autonomic nervous system, which controls involuntary bodily functions such as your heart rate and stress responses. Box breathing reduces the fight-or-flight response, promoting a sense of calm and stability. The breath-hold phases allow carbon dioxide levels to build slightly, which can activate your vagus nerve, enhancing relaxation.[4]

Practicing box breathing is simple and can be done anywhere. Begin by standing or sitting in a comfortable position with a straight spine and relaxed shoulders. Inhale slowly through the nose for a count of four, feeling your lungs fill completely. Hold your breath for another count of four, maintaining a relaxed but firm hold. Exhale gently and completely through the mouth for four counts, releasing any tension. Finally, pause before inhaling and hold your breath again for four counts before starting the cycle anew.

Coherent Breathing (Resonance Breathing)

Coherent breathing, also known as resonance breathing, involves maintaining a steady and controlled breathing rate of approximately five to six breaths per minute. This technique enhances heart rate variability (HRV), which is the natural variation of time between each heartbeat. Higher HRV is associated with improved emotional regulation, reduced stress, and increased resilience. Studies indicate that this technique not only promotes relaxation but also fosters a balanced state within the autonomic nervous system, leading to greater emotional stability and mental clarity.[5]

To practice coherent breathing, find a comfortable seated or lying position where you can relax your muscles. Begin by inhaling slowly and deeply through your nose for a count of six seconds, allowing your belly to expand gently. Without pausing, exhale slowly through your nose or mouth for another count of six seconds. The goal is to maintain this balanced breathing pattern, focusing on the smooth transition between inhales and exhales. You may find it helpful to visualize the breath as a gentle wave, rising and falling in a consistent rhythm.

Alternate Nostril Breathing (Nadi Shodhana)

Alternate nostril breathing, known in yoga as Nadi Shodhana, is a practice that involves controlled breathing through one nostril at a time while blocking the opposite nostril. This method is traditionally used to balance the flow of energy in the body, but modern research highlights its physiological benefits, including improved autonomic balance, reduced anxiety, and enhanced cognitive clarity.[6]

To practice alternate nostril breathing, sit comfortably with a straight spine. Using your right thumb, gently close your right nostril. Inhale slowly and deeply through your left nostril, focusing on a smooth, even breath. At the peak of your inhale, close your left nostril with your ring and pinky fingers while simultaneously releasing your right nostril. Exhale slowly through the right nostril. Next, inhale through the right nostril, close it with your thumb, and exhale through the left nostril. This completes one full cycle. Five cycles are generally recommended, or you can continue alternating sides, maintaining a steady, relaxed breathing rhythm for five to ten minutes.

Extended Exhalation Breathing

Extended exhalation breathing is a technique that emphasizes lengthening the exhale in relation to the inhale. For example, you might inhale for four counts and exhale for six or more counts. This method also activates the parasympathetic nervous system, which promotes a state of relaxation by increasing vagal tone. Higher vagal tone is associated with greater resilience to stress and improved emotional regulation.

To practice extended exhalation breathing, find a comfortable seated or lying position. Begin by taking a deep, gentle inhale through your nose for a count of four. Focus on filling your lungs fully, allowing your belly to rise. Then, exhale slowly through your mouth or nose for a count of six (or longer), ensuring the breath remains smooth and controlled. You can gradually increase the length of your exhalation as you become more comfortable with the practice.

Implementing Breathwork

Mr. Carter

Mr. Carter, a special education teacher, stands at the front of his classroom, guiding the morning routine with practiced ease. His classroom is thoughtfully designed to support his neurodiverse students. Soft lighting reduces sensory overload, noise-canceling headphones are readily available, and flexible seating options encourage movement and comfort.

As Mr. Carter begins reviewing the date and weather, an unexpected trigger sets off a chain reaction. A high-pitched scream from one student pierces the air, and another student, agitated, begins dragging her desk across the floor, creating a loud screech. The noise reverberates through the room, overwhelming a student with auditory sensitivity, who immediately presses his hands to his ears and begins to cry. Another student, anxious and distressed by the escalating chaos, repeats "Stop it" rapidly and with rising intensity.

Although these disruptions are not necessarily unusual, Mr. Carter has an important IEP meeting scheduled, and dealing with multiple student escalations simultaneously will almost certainly consume the extra time he needs to prepare. Mr. Carter notices his mind racing as the urgency of the situation becomes clear. His pulse quickens, his chest tightens, and he has an immediate impulse to call for assistance. Recognizing that he is having an automatic stress response, Mr. Carter decides to engage with a self-regulation strategy before making any decisions.

He pauses, takes a breath, and begins box breathing. He straightens his posture, inhaling through his nose for four counts, holding for four, exhaling slowly through his mouth for four counts, and holding again for four counts. As he continues the cycle, he feels his heartbeat slow down, and his thoughts begin to settle. With each breath, the noise of the classroom recedes slightly, and his composure returns. In less than two minutes, his mind is no longer clouded by stress; he is present and in control.

Now, calm and clear, Mr. Carter moves into action with a focused strategy. He calmly directs his paraprofessional to implement the Behavior Intervention Plan (BIP) for the student who is screaming, confident that this will help de-escalate the situation. Meanwhile, he moves toward the student who is dragging the desk and gently holds up the visual prompt that signals "sit quietly." He offers noise-canceling headphones to the students who might need them, giving each student a high-five when they make an effort to stay calm or use the headphones.

(Continued)

(Continued)

Key Considerations: Mr. Carter

Mr. Carter's experience illustrates how breathwork can serve as a quick and highly effective tool for managing stress in the fast-paced, high-pressure environment of a special education classroom. In moments of heightened stress, particularly when dealing with sensory overload and emotional dysregulation in students, your ability to remain composed and make intentional decisions is critical.

By consistently practicing controlled breathing techniques, Mr. Carter reinforces the connection between his prefrontal cortex, the brain's center for decision-making and emotional control, and his autonomic nervous system, which governs involuntary bodily functions like heart rate.

Over time, breathwork strengthens Mr. Carter's capacity to maintain composure, adapt to the needs of his students, and make strategic decisions in real-time.

Technological Options for Breathwork

Breathwork offers structured breathing exercises for relaxation, focus, and sleep.

Othership provides guided breathwork sessions with music for emotional regulation.

HeartMath Inner Balance uses HRV biofeedback to optimize breathing and stress management.

Muse tracks brainwave activity and breath patterns.

Oura Ring monitors HRV, sleep, and respiration for breathwork insights.

Airofit enhances lung capacity and breathing control, used by athletes and health professionals.

Moonbird is a handheld device that provides real-time biofeedback for paced breathing.

Implementing Breathwork With Technology

Ms. Ramirez

Ms. Ramirez, a special education paraprofessional, supports a group of students with intellectual disabilities. Today, one of her students, Marcus, struggled with a new transition routine. When it was time to move from lunch to the classroom, Marcus resisted, becoming visibly anxious and upset. He clenched his fists, stomped his feet, and eventually sat down in the hallway, refusing to move. Ms. Ramirez presented a visual schedule and gave Marcus extra time to process the transition. However, Marcus continued to escalate, eventually screaming and hitting himself around his head. With the help of the classroom teacher, Ms. Ramirez was able to guide him back to the classroom, but the experience left her feeling emotionally drained and tense.

Ms. Ramirez asked to take her fifteen-minute break and found a quiet place to use her HeartMath Inner Balance device, which helps regulate stress by providing real-time heart rate variability (HRV) biofeedback. She clips the sensor to her earlobe, opens the companion app on her phone, and begins following the guided breathing exercise. The app provides visual cues for inhaling and exhaling at an optimal rhythm, helping her synchronize her breath with her heart rate. As she breathes in deeply and exhales slowly, the app indicates that her HRV is improving, signaling a shift into a more balanced state.

(Continued)

(Continued)

The tension in her shoulders dissipates, and she feels her mind settle. After a few minutes, she notices that she's no longer replaying the moment with Marcus in her head. Instead, she feels more grounded, reminding herself that Marcus's response was part of his learning process, and she begins to jot down potential interventions for future classroom transitions.

Key Considerations: Ms. Ramirez

Ms. Ramirez's experience illustrates how technology can provide educators with an additional layer of support for self-regulation strategies. Special education staff often face unpredictable, high-stakes situations, and while traditional breathwork techniques are notably effective, biofeedback tools like HeartMath Inner Balance offer objective data that reinforces the effectiveness of breathwork in real-time.

Studies on HRV biofeedback suggest that using real-time physiological data can significantly improve your emotional regulation and stress resilience.[7]

By integrating this technology into her routine, Ms. Ramirez is not just managing stress in the moment. She is actively training her nervous system to recover more efficiently from emotionally demanding situations. From a neuroplasticity perspective, breathwork combined with biofeedback helps rewire stress responses by strengthening the brain's ability to shift from high-alert states to calm, regulated states more efficiently.

COGNITIVE REFRAMING

Tool Number Two: Cognitive Reframing

When a meeting takes an unexpected turn or a classroom erupts into chaos, stress can rise quickly, leading to reactions that feel automatic and difficult to control. Cognitive reframing provides a practical and effective method for reinterpreting these experiences. This tool allows you to move from a reactive state to a more thoughtful and balanced mindset.

Cognitive reframing is a well-researched self-regulation tool that actively changes how your brain processes stress.[8] It does this by engaging your brain's capacity to *reinterpret* challenges through a more constructive lens. This process begins by identifying automatic responses, questioning their validity, and consciously choosing more constructive interpretations.

The consistent use of this technique not only enhances your emotional control immediately, but also reinforces neural pathways that promote long-term resilience. When you see difficulties from a different perspective, you can transform stress into a source of strength while maintaining composure and effectiveness, even in the most demanding environments.

Techniques for Cognitive Reframing

Socratic Questioning

This technique involves challenging automatic negative thoughts by systematically questioning their validity. For example, when a negative thought comes up, ask: What evidence supports this thought? What evidence contradicts it? Am I assuming the worst possible outcome? How would I advise a colleague in the same situation?

By engaging in this structured questioning, you weaken the influence of cognitive distortions and create space for more balanced interpretations. Studies on cognitive-behavioral therapy (CBT) show that Socratic questioning is an effective method for modifying thought patterns and enhancing problem-solving abilities.[9]

Imagine Sarah, an adaptive P.E. coach, feels discouraged after a challenging meeting. She thinks, *"I'm failing at my job. Everyone sees it."* Instead of accepting this thought as fact, she takes a moment to engage in the following dialogue internally or by writing it down as follows:

1. What evidence supports this thought? *Answer*: I felt tense during the meeting and noticed that a colleague disagreed with my approach.

2. What evidence contradicts it? *Answer*: Other team members complimented my teaching strategies last week, and I recently helped a colleague successfully implement a new curriculum.

3. Am I assuming the worst possible outcome? *Answer*: Yes. I am actually reacting to one disagreement as if it defines my entire performance.

4. How would I advise a colleague in the same situation? *Answer*: I would remind them that one meeting and one person does not reflect overall competence and that constructive disagreement is part of collaboration.

By systematically questioning her automatic thought, Sarah recognizes that her belief of "failing" lacks firm evidence. She reinterprets the situation as a normal exchange of ideas instead of a sign of inadequacy, allowing her to move forward with confidence.

Perspective Shifting

This approach encourages you to step outside of your immediate viewpoint and consider alternative ways of interpreting an event. This may involve asking, How might my student, their parents, or a colleague perceive this situation? By actively considering different perspectives, you develop cognitive flexibility, reducing your emotional reactivity and increasing the ability to navigate complex interactions with greater empathy and understanding.

Consider Joan, a special educator, who has just finished a challenging meeting with a parent. She leaves the discussion feeling tense. Her shoulders are stiff, and she's replaying the parent's criticisms in her head. The parent seemed frustrated about the child's progress and was very critical of Joan's interventions. Initially, Joan started questioning her competence. But instead of allowing these thoughts about her ability to continue, she engages in a quick perspective-taking exercise by jotting down the following:

1. How might the parent see this situation? *Answer:* She could be worried that her child is falling behind or not receiving the individual support needed. Her frustration might come from a place of fear or helplessness.

2. How would my colleagues view this interaction? *Answer:* They would likely recognize the parent's comments were harsh, but they would probably view the intensity as a sign of concern, not hostility, and they might encourage me to place greater emphasis on the progress that has been made and my willingness to try new strategies.

3. If I were a neutral observer, how would I view this? *Answer:* I would notice two people who both care about the student's well-being but need clearer communication and a shared plan.

By exploring these alternative viewpoints, Joan realizes that the parent's critical tone may stem from genuine worry, and her comments arose from frustration, and not Joan's competence. She feels her initial tension easing and gains empathy for the parent's concerns. This allows her to consider fresh approaches for collaborating on her student's academic and emotional needs.

Positive Attribution

Any setback you encounter can either reinforce feelings of defeat or encourage growth. It is natural to personalize classroom challenges. When something doesn't work, our first instinct is often to assume we've missed the mark in some way. But instead of attributing challenges to personal failure, you can choose to reframe them as opportunities for professional learning and student development. For example, rather than thinking, "I could not engage my student today. I must be doing something wrong," a reframed thought might be, "My student struggled to engage today. I may need to think about my approach and different ways to increase engagement." This shift moves you from self-criticism to problem-solving, opening up possibilities for new strategies and a deeper understanding of your students' needs.

Cognitive Distancing

This technique recognizes that thoughts are not absolute truths but rather mental interpretations open to adjustment. Instead of automatically reacting to stressful thoughts, you can practice detachment and neutral observation. For example, instead of thinking, "I'll never be able to manage this student's behavior," you might consider, "I am having the thought that I can't manage this situation right now, but that doesn't mean this is true."

By labeling thoughts as transient mental events rather than facts, you reduce emotional reactivity and create space for more balanced perspectives.

Emotional Regulation Scripts

Scripts provide a structured, preprepared language to guide you through moments of stress, frustration, or self-doubt. Unlike cognitive reframing, which requires real-time analysis and restructuring of thoughts, ER scripts offer an immediate verbal framework for managing emotions effectively. These scripts typically follow a structured pattern: acknowledging the emotional response, validating the experience, and providing a calming or perspective-shifting statement.

For example, John, an occupational therapist, is engaged in a group session where multiple students need his attention at the same time. The intensity is rising with only seven minutes left until the session ends. As John's anxiety builds, he remembers his three-step script and quickly engages (mentally) in the following:

1. Acknowledge the Feeling: "I am feeling really anxious right now. I feel my heart beating faster and tightness in my shoulders."

2. Validate the Experience: "It makes sense to feel this way because several students are asking for help simultaneously, and I'm worried I won't have enough time to meet everyone's needs before the session ends."

3. Provide a Calming Statement: "I've successfully handled urgent situations in the past, and I know I can do it again. I'll take three deep belly breaths right now to center myself, then address each student in a calm, focused way. If I run out of time, I will begin where I left off next time."

This structured practice helps John regain composure and effectively manage the group session despite the time constraints.

Implementing Cognitive Reframing

Ms. Bennett

Ms. Bennett, a special education supervisor, just finished an IEP meeting that left her feeling overwhelmed. The meeting did not go as planned. The student's parents were visibly upset, questioning whether the school and district were providing enough support and threatening to hire an attorney.

Although she remained professional, Ms. Bennett left the meeting feeling criticized, their comments echoing in her mind. She was new to her leadership role, and a voice inside kept insisting that she was failing as a supervisor and she might be failing the student as well.

Before heading home, Ms. Bennett sat at her desk and opened her notepad. She began by writing her thoughts exactly as they appeared. Recognizing a familiar pattern of self-blame, she first engaged in Socratic questioning by asking herself, "What evidence supports the belief that I am failing, and what evidence contradicts this thought?" Her answers revealed that the only evidence that she was failing the student was the parent's remarks throughout the meeting. Data clearly showed significant improvement in seven out of ten goals, and team members had thanked her for her advocacy and support, which are important components of a supervisor's role. Both of these facts contradicted the belief that she was failing.

Next, she practiced perspective shifting by considering how the parents might view the situation. The parents seemed to disregard the areas of improvement and focused almost exclusively on their child's reading goal, which showed very little progress. She considered that the parents' frustration might stem from a deep concern about how a lack of reading skills impacts all subject areas. From that perspective, the parents were not judging her professional abilities. The primary concern was the child's challenges with reading and comprehension, which is bound to create challenges across all subject areas.

Ms. Bennett then applied positive attribution by reframing the setback as an opportunity for growth. Rather than interpreting the parents' frustration as a personal failure, she recognized it as a valid frustration over her child's struggle with reading and comprehension. From this perspective, Ms. Bennett decides to collaborate with her team to research additional reading programs and strategies that might help the student's progress.

Through these cognitive reframing techniques, Ms. Bennett not only processed the emotional challenges constructively, she also reinforced the mental resilience needed for future conversations and developed a plan to address a legitimate concern.

Key Considerations: Ms. Bennett

Ms. Bennett's experience underscores how cognitive reframing can break the cycle of automatic self-doubt. Human brains naturally give greater attention to negative information, a phenomenon known as the negativity bias, primarily driven by the amygdala.[9]

Left unchallenged, repeated stress strengthens these negative pathways, causing self-criticism to become habitual. However, by employing techniques such as Socratic questioning, perspective-shifting, and positive attribution, you can interrupt this cycle and shift self-doubt to problem-solving. This lessens the emotional impact of challenging situations and paves the way for solutions that align with your long-term goals.

Technological Tools for Cognitive Reframing

CBT Thought Record apps like *Sanvello* and *CBT Thought Diary* guide users through structured cognitive reframing exercises based on cognitive behavioral therapy (CBT). They help users identify negative thought patterns, challenge distortions, and develop healthier perspectives.

AI-Powered Journaling platforms like *Woebot* use conversational AI to engage users in real-time cognitive reframing by questioning unhelpful thought patterns and providing psychoeducational support.

Virtual Reality (VR) platforms like *TRIPP* offer immersive experiences designed to shift emotional perspectives, reduce stress, and promote cognitive flexibility. VR-based cognitive interventions have been found to help reframe anxiety-inducing situations and train the brain in adaptive stress responses.

Implementing Cognitive Reframing With Technology

Mr. Harris

Mr. Harris, a middle school special education teacher, had a difficult morning. During science, one of his students, Daniel, a bright and thoughtful learner with an intellectual disability, shut down completely. When Mr. Harris gently encouraged

(Continued)

(Continued)

Key Considerations: Mr. Harris

Mr. Harris's experience shows the potential of technology to provide structured, evidence-based guidance in unsettling moments.

Special educators deeply care about the students they serve, and many, like Mr. Harris, immediately question themselves when students struggle academically or behaviorally. Using cognitive reframing apps helps guide you to realistic expectations for yourself, your students, and your staff members. These apps also offer a practical way to interrupt negative thought patterns when time for self-reflection is limited.

GROUNDING

Tool Number Three: Grounding

Have you ever paused during your workday, feeling truly present in that moment? The demands of a special educator often require you to focus on many things at once, and this often leads to emotional overwhelm and a feeling of disconnection. By bringing your attention to the present moment, grounding exercises can rapidly create stability and a renewed sense of focus. Grounding strategies direct your attention outward, prompting you to focus on sensations like your feet against the floor, the ambient sounds in the room, or the subtle aroma of your surroundings. While cognitive reframing shifts thought patterns, grounding shifts your focus and interrupts reactivity so that you can regulate your emotions quickly.

Types of Grounding

- *Sensory-based grounding* involves actively engaging one or more of the five senses. This might include touching a textured object, feeling the rhythm of breath, listening to surrounding sounds, or noticing distinct scents or tastes. Research suggests that multi-sensory engagement reduces activation in the amygdala, helping the brain return to a state of regulation. Sensory input stimulates different neural pathways, helping override distressing emotions and bringing awareness back to the present.[10]

- *Cognitive grounding* uses structured mental exercises to redirect focus. This can include naming objects in the environment, mentally listing factual details, or repeating a neutral or calming phrase. By engaging the executive functioning system of the brain, cognitive grounding disrupts overwhelming thoughts and facilitates emotional regulation.

By the end of a grounding exercise, the nervous system shifts toward a more regulated state. The body and mind become more centered, allowing for clearer thinking and a calmer emotional response.

Techniques for Grounding

Sensory Awareness (5-4-3-2-1)

This simple yet powerful technique engages all five senses to shift your focus away from emotional distress and into the present moment. First, pause and take a moment to identify five things you see, four things you can touch, three things that you hear, two things you can smell, and one thing you can taste. Repeat this exercise, choosing different answers until you feel fully present.

Physical Grounding Objects

To effectively use physical grounding, find a space where you will not be interrupted for a few minutes, then choose a textured object that feels appealing to you. This could be a smooth stone, a soft piece of fabric, or a stress ball. Hold the object in your hand and close your eyes if preferred. Focus on the object's details: Notice its temperature, texture, weight, and any subtle contours or imperfections. Allow your fingers to explore the surface, paying close attention to the sensations elicited by each touch.

As you immerse yourself in this sensory experience, gently redirect your focus away from distressing thoughts and focus on the object in your hand.

Let the tactile information anchor you in the present moment. The sensation of touch stimulates the somatosensory cortex, reinforcing your focus on physical reality rather than emotional distress.

Feet on the Floor Exercise

Begin by positioning yourself comfortably (either seated or standing) in a quiet space where you can focus without interruption. Place both feet flat on the floor, ensuring full contact with the surface beneath you. Slowly press your feet firmly into the ground and direct your attention to the sensations that emerge. Feel the steady pressure and the reassuring support that your feet provide. Notice how the solidity of the floor conveys a sense of stability and grounding.

As you maintain this deliberate pressure, allow your breathing to slow and deepen naturally. Focus on the connection between your feet and the floor, letting this sensory input anchor you in the present moment. This mindful engagement activates your proprioceptive awareness, reinforcing a sense of control and immediate stability.

Verbal Grounding Statements

Verbal grounding uses clear, factual statements to anchor your awareness in the present moment. You can use this tool in a quiet space or in real time. In either setting, begin by taking a few deep, slow breaths to center your mind. Then, state a fact like, "I am in my office, it is 3:00 p.m., and I am sitting in a chair," clearly and deliberately. For added reinforcement, you might include additional objective details: "I am wearing a blue shirt and black pants; natural sunlight illuminates the room; and I can hear the soft hum of the air conditioner." As you enunciate each detail, your focus shifts from emotional distress to the concrete reality around you. Speaking a factual, neutral statement aloud interrupts emotional reactivity and helps engage the logical processing centers of the brain.

Implementing Grounding

Ms. Reynolds

Ms. Reynolds, a special education teacher, felt emotionally overwhelmed after a tense conversation with her school principal regarding a parent phone call. Though she maintained her professionalism, the intensity of the exchange left her unsettled and struggling to refocus on her next task. Before stepping back into her classroom, she paused to engage in a verbal grounding exercise.

Ms. Reynolds began her grounding practice by taking slow, deliberate breaths. She clearly and deliberately stated a factual description of her present situation: "I am in the school building, it is 2:30 p.m., and I am preparing to teach." For added reinforcement, she continued, "I am wearing my favorite shoes and they feel soft and comfortable; the room is filled with natural light, and I can hear the soft murmur of colleagues in the background." As she enunciated these objective details, her focus shifted away from the emotional distress of the earlier conversation to the concrete reality of the present moment. She felt a restored sense of calm as she entered the classroom.

Key Considerations: Ms. Reynolds

Ms. Reynolds's experience shows how grounding can defuse intense emotions quickly, which helps her to remain composed after an intense discussion. By naming what she saw and felt around her, she shifted attention from a rush of internal distress to the steady, concrete details of her surroundings. That outward focus interrupted the spiral of negative feeling and allowed her thinking brain to regain control.

Grounding only takes a few moments, but the results are significant. Just a few moments of describing sights, sounds, and textures can help the nervous system settle. These techniques can be invaluable for special educators, who regularly confront stressful situations throughout their day.

Technological Tools for Grounding

Guided Grounding apps, such as *Insight Timer* and *Calm*, provide structured grounding exercises, guiding users through sensory-based or cognitive grounding techniques to regulate emotions.

Biofeedback Wearables like *Apollo Neuro* and *HeartMath Inner Balance* monitor physiological stress markers and provide real-time feedback, helping users engage in grounding exercises at the first signs of emotional escalation.

Haptic Feedback Devices like *TouchPoints* use gentle vibrations to create rhythmic stimulation, providing an external sensory anchor to help regulate emotions.

Implementing Grounding With Technology

Mr. Hayes

Mr. Hayes, a school psychologist, spends his day supporting students in crisis, often shifting from one emotionally intense conversation to another. Today, he met with a student experiencing extreme anxiety, and though the session was productive, he feels the residual tension weighing on him. He has learned that if he does not take time to regulate between sessions, his stress levels build throughout the day, affecting his ability to remain fully present.

Before heading into his next meeting, he puts on his Apollo Neuro wearable, which provides rhythmic vibrations designed to support relaxation. He opens the companion app and selects a setting for stress reduction. As the gentle pulses activate his sense of touch, he pairs the experience with a guided grounding session from the Calm app, which walks him through sensory awareness techniques. The structured guidance helps him focus on external stimuli; first, the weight of his body against the chair, then the sensation of his breath moving in and out. After a few minutes, he feels the lingering stress begin to dissipate. His breathing is steadier, and his thoughts are clearer. He turns off the app and heads into his next session, feeling more balanced.

Key Considerations: Mr. Hayes

Mr. Hayes's experience illustrates how technology-assisted grounding provides structured, real-time support for emotional regulation in high-stress professional settings. For individuals in emotionally demanding roles, accumulating stress between interactions can undermine their presence and effectiveness.

Wearable devices that deliver rhythmic, calming vibrations serve as external anchors that help regulate the nervous system through sensory pathways. Research shows that this kind of haptic feedback can move people from a heightened stress response to a more regulated state.[11] Paired with structured grounding prompts in an app, the tactile cue steadies the body while the prompts guide attention back to the present moment.

PROGRESSIVE MUSCLE RELAXATION

Tool Number Four: Progressive Muscle Relaxation

After a long day of navigating unpredictable challenges, your body may feel like a tightly coiled spring. Your shoulders may be tense, your jaw clenched, or your muscles heavy from stress. Progressive Muscle Relaxation (PMR) gives you a way to release the physical weight of the day and restore a sense of calm.

PMR is a self-regulation tool that systematically tenses and releases different muscle groups to reduce physical tension and promote emotional calm. Unlike passive relaxation, which simply encourages stillness, PMR actively engages your body to signal safety to the nervous system. The practice involves sequentially contracting and relaxing your muscles, typically starting at the feet and moving upward through your body. By deliberately tightening muscles and then releasing them, you develop a greater awareness of physical tension, allowing you to consciously let go of stress.

Research indicates that PMR not only reduces muscle tension but also lowers cortisol levels, enhances vagal tone, and improves emotional resilience.[12] Because stress is often stored in the body, engaging in regular PMR helps break cycles of chronic tension, allowing you to feel more present, grounded, and emotionally balanced in your role.

PMR follows a structured sequence. The process begins by finding a quiet, comfortable space where distractions are minimal. Sitting or lying down in a relaxed position also helps with the practice.

Techniques for PMR

Classic Progressive Muscle Relaxation

Edmund Jacobson developed PMR in 1938.[13] This structured approach involves systematically tensing and relaxing muscle groups, promoting relaxation, and reducing stress. It remains the gold standard for PMR techniques.

1. Begin by bringing awareness to your body, noticing any areas of tension or discomfort. Start with the feet and move upward, tensing each muscle group for a few seconds. After holding the tension briefly, fully release the muscles. Continue this sequence through the legs, abdomen, chest, arms, shoulders, neck, and face.

2. Practice slow, deep breathing throughout the practice to enhance relaxation. For example, breathe in deeply as you tense the muscles in your feet, then exhale and release the muscle group simultaneously. Using conscious breathing while engaged in PMR strengthens the mind-body connection, reinforcing the brain's ability to transition from stress to calm.

3. After completing the full-body sequence, it may be helpful to take a moment of stillness to allow the body to settle into relaxation.

With regular practice, your body learns to recognize tension earlier and release it more efficiently, making PMR a powerful tool for long-term stress regulation.

Body Scanning and PMR

This variation integrates mindfulness with muscle relaxation by shifting the focus from actively tensing your muscles to observing your bodily sensations. Begin by sitting or lying in a quiet space and closing your eyes. Direct your attention slowly, from your toes upward to your head, observing areas of tightness or discomfort, but avoid deliberately tensing your muscles. Instead, acknowledge these sensations and allow them to ease naturally.

PMR for Sleep

Using PMR as part of a bedtime routine can significantly enhance your sleep quality, which naturally results in a positive impact on your workday. Prepare your sleeping environment by dimming the lights and minimizing distractions. While lying in bed, begin the standard PMR sequence from your feet upward, focusing on slow, deep breathing as you release tension in each muscle group. This process helps your body transition from a state of alertness to one of relaxation, thereby improving sleep onset, duration, and quality, especially for those with stress-related insomnia.

Implementing PMR

Ms. Lawson

Ms. Lawson, a special education paraprofessional, feels the accumulated stress of a demanding school day. Her shoulders ache from leaning over desks, and her back is sore from physically assisting students with medical needs.

After dismissal, Ms. Lawson finds a quiet space outside and sits on a bench to begin a progressive muscle relaxation session. She starts at her feet, inhaling slowly and deeply as she deliberately tenses her calf muscles. Holding the breath and the contraction for a few moments, she then exhales fully, releasing the tension and inviting a wave of relaxation. Moving upward, she applies this method to each muscle group. She clenches her fists with a deep inhalation, pausing briefly, and then letting go on a long exhale, followed by lifting her shoulders toward her ears on the next inhalation and letting them fall as she exhales.

As she continues this deliberate pattern from her legs, through her abdomen, chest, and arms, and finally reaching her neck and face, the combination of focused breathing and targeted muscle release creates a potent transition. Each exhale releases layers of stress, while every inhale fortifies her connection between mind and body. By the time she gently tenses and relaxes the muscles around her jaw and forehead, the tight knots of tension begin to dissolve, and a subtle calm takes over. The process takes less than ten minutes.

Key Considerations: Ms. Lawson

Ms. Lawson's experience highlights how progressive muscle relaxation provides a quick body-based strategy for releasing stress. Special education professionals often carry the emotional and physical weight of their roles without realizing how much tension accumulates in their muscles. Without intentional release, this tension can build and contribute to chronic stress, fatigue, and burnout.

From a neuroplasticity perspective, repeatedly practicing progressive muscle relaxation strengthens the brain's ability to recognize and release tension before it becomes overwhelming. By regularly engaging in this practice, Ms. Lawson is rewiring her nervous system to shift into a relaxed state more efficiently, reducing her overall stress load. Over time, this not only enhances her emotional well-being but also improves her ability to remain present, patient, and physically at ease in her work with students.

Technological Tools for PMR

Guided PMR Apps like *Calm* and *Insight Timer* provide structured PMR sessions with verbal guidance, helping users maintain focus and consistency in their practice.

Biofeedback wearables like *HeartMath Inner Balance* and *Oura Ring* track heart rate variability (HRV), offering real-time physiological feedback that allows users to measure the effectiveness of their PMR practice.

Smart wearables for stress monitoring, such as *Apollo Neuro* and *Fitbit*, detect changes in skin conductance and HRV, helping users recognize when to engage in PMR based on their body's stress response.

VR-Based Relaxation Programs like *TRIPP VR* provide immersive PMR experiences that deepen the relaxation response by integrating visual and auditory cues that reinforce the muscle relaxation process.

Sleep-Tracking Devices with PMR Integration include *Whoop* and *Oura Ring* to assess sleep stages and recovery, helping users evaluate the impact of PMR on sleep quality and overall nervous system recovery.

Implementing PMR With Technology

Mr. Blake

Mr. Blake, a speech-language pathologist working in a special education setting, carries a great deal of physical tension throughout the day. Between back-to-back therapy sessions, progress monitoring, and difficult conversations with parents, his body feels rigid, and his stress levels remain high. He has noticed that even when he gets home, his body is still on high alert, making it difficult to fully unwind.

During a break between sessions, he uses the Calm app, which offers a short, guided progressive muscle relaxation exercise. He puts on his headphones, finds a quiet space, and follows the audio prompts. The voice guides him through a structured sequence, instructing him to tighten each muscle group and release it, bringing his awareness to how relaxation feels in his body. He follows along as the voice directs him to tense his legs, hold the contraction, and let go. With each release, his breathing slows, his heart rate decreases, and he feels his body settling into a state of calm. By the end of the session, he feels less drained and more present, ready to engage with his next student with renewed energy.

Key Considerations: Mr. Blake

Mr. Blake's experience highlights the added value of technology in facilitating progressive muscle relaxation. By using a guided app, he accesses a structured and consistent approach that not only helps him release physical tension but also supports a regular practice even amidst a hectic schedule. Guided PMR interventions reinforce neural pathways associated with stress regulation. Over time, this consistent engagement can improve emotional regulation, decrease physical strain, and build resilience, enabling professionals like Mr. Blake to maintain focus and energy in their demanding roles.

DIALECTICAL BEHAVIOR THERAPY (DBT-INFORMED STRATEGIES)

Tool Number Five: DBT-Informed Strategies

In high-stakes moments when emotional intensity builds, your body may tense, your thoughts may fragment, and a familiar wave of urgency can set in. DBT-Informed Strategies give you a way to interrupt that cycle, regain internal balance, and respond with composure.

Many of the tools discussed earlier in this chapter, including breathwork, cognitive reframing, and progressive muscle relaxation, are embedded throughout DBT's full framework. However, Dialectical Behavior Therapy (DBT) is a comprehensive, evidence-based treatment developed by Dr. Marsha Linehan to support individuals experiencing chronic emotional dysregulation.[14] It is widely used in clinical settings through a structured curriculum that includes training in mindfulness, distress tolerance, emotion regulation, and interpersonal effectiveness. This model requires extensive professional training, clinical oversight, and a commitment to fidelity in implementation.

Although DBT is rooted in clinical care, select strategies have been adapted for broader use. In particular, techniques from the distress tolerance category offer fast-acting tools that can be used by professionals in high-stress environments. These practices are not replacements for clinical DBT. They represent only a narrow portion of the complete framework and are shared here solely as accessible, research-informed strategies to assist educators and related service providers in managing acute emotional responses.

The following DBT-informed techniques are most effective in real-time, especially when the nervous system is highly activated. These tools help disrupt reactivity, calm the body's stress response, and allow space for executive function to re-engage. For professionals in special education, these techniques can be instrumental in preserving composure and responding with intention.

Techniques for DBT-Informed Strategies

The STOP Method

The STOP method helps interrupt reactive behavior by guiding the individual through a structured internal sequence. The steps include:

S (Stop): Freeze the action. Do not move. Do not speak. Do not react.

T (Take a step back): Physically, mentally, and/or emotionally pause and detach from the heat of the moment.

O (Observe): Notice what is happening internally and externally. What are you feeling? What triggered this? What thoughts are forming?

P (Proceed mindfully): Act with awareness, not from automatic emotion. Choose what aligns with your values and the current situation.

For example, let's say a student throws a chair during a media center rotation. First, you would **Stop**: Your hands stay at your sides. Your voice stays quiet. You make no move to intervene just yet. Everything in you pauses. Then you **Take a step back** by pulling your attention inward for just a second. Physically, you soften your stance. Mentally, you allow space between the behavior and your first impulse. You are not detaching from the student. You are giving your nervous system a chance to regulate. Next, you simply **Observe**: You feel your pulse in your neck. Your throat is tight. The student is now crying and pushing papers off the table. You see your para-professional waiting for a cue. You identify what is happening inside you—urgency, embarrassment, and a rising need to fix it. You notice it all, but you do not act yet. When you **Proceed**, you do it mindfully: You exhale slowly. You remember that this student struggles most after unstructured activities. Your next step is not about stopping the behavior. It is about restoring safety. You signal your paraprofessional to initiate the calm corner protocol. You kneel next to the student, using few words and an open posture.

Each element of the STOP technique supports the shift from limbic reactivity to executive functioning. By pausing and observing without immediate reaction, the brain reengages cognitive processing, allowing for thoughtful and appropriate responses. This technique is particularly effective when facing unexpected disruptions or emotionally charged interactions.

The TIPP Method

TIPP stands for Temperature, Intense Exercise, Paced Breathing, Progressive Muscle Relaxation. This technique offers a set of immediate physiological interventions that target the body's stress response and reduce emotional arousal by quickly changing your internal states. Each step is briefly described below:

- *Temperature:* Exposure to cold, such as splashing cold water on the face or holding an ice pack, activates the dive reflex, which slows the heart rate and reduces sympathetic nervous system arousal.[15]

- *Intense Exercise:* Short bursts of high-intensity movement (jumping jacks, running in place, brisk walking) help discharge adrenaline and reduce emotional overwhelm.

- *Paced Breathing:* Intentional, slow breathing reduces hyperarousal and engages the parasympathetic nervous system. A common method is breathing in for four counts and out for six.

- *Progressive Muscle Relaxation:* As noted previously, PMR involves systematically tensing and releasing muscle groups to reduce physical tension and signal safety to the nervous system.

Let's say you are a behavior interventionist who spent almost thirty minutes tracking a neurodiverse student who left the school building and tried to climb the fence surrounding the school. Your school is in a high-traffic area, so the stress and fear were intense and remain with you, even when the student eventually returned to his classroom. Using the TIPP Method, you might go into the teacher's lounge and splash cold water on your face from the nearby sink (Temperature), then jog in place for twenty seconds to release the adrenaline (Intense Exercise). Now you can slow your breath, inhaling for four counts and exhaling for six (Paced Breathing). Finally, you can tense and release your hands and shoulders (Progressive Muscle Relaxation). In less than five minutes, your system begins to settle, and you are ready to tackle your next task, clear-headed and composed.

Implementing DBT-Informed Strategies

Key Considerations: Ms. Jones

Ms. Jones's ability to stay grounded during an escalating situation reflects a well-integrated self-regulation response. By engaging the STOP sequence, she interrupts her body's initial fight or flight reaction and shifts neural activity from the limbic system to the prefrontal cortex.[16] This redirection enables her to respond with intention rather than impulse.

Her physical stillness at the doorway reduces sympathetic arousal and signals safety to both her nervous system and those around her. Noticing physical sensations without acting on them activates interoceptive awareness, a function supported by the anterior insula.[17] This brain region plays a role in identifying internal states and contributes to emotional regulation.

Each component of the STOP process strengthens executive functions such as inhibition, flexible thinking, and perspective taking. By the time Ms. Jones engages the student, her actions reflect clarity and composure. This not only supports immediate de-escalation but also communicates calm authority and creates a foundation of psychological safety. Repeated use of this strategy builds resilience and reinforces neural pathways that support effective leadership during high-stress encounters.

Technological Tools for DBT-Informed Strategies

DBT Coach offers real-time practice with STOP and TIPP strategies through interactive reminders and digital prompts.

Implementing DBT-Informed Strategies With Technology

Mr. Tyler

Mr. Tyler, a middle school paraprofessional, steps into an empty office after assisting in the aftermath of a hallway altercation. His chest feels tight, his hands are trembling, and he is struggling to calm down. He recalls a recent training about the TIPP strategy, but due to his current state, he cannot remember all of the steps. He opens the DBT Coach app on his phone and selects the Distress Tolerance module. The screen offers a list of strategies, and he taps on TIPP. The app explains each component, prompting him to begin with a temperature-based strategy.

He retrieves a cold pack from the nurse's freezer, presses it gently to his face, and holds it there for thirty seconds. Next, the app suggests movement. He completes a brief set of wall push-ups, focusing on his breath. The app provides instructions and a timer for paced breathing, so he follows along, inhaling for four counts and exhaling for six. The final prompt walks him through progressive muscle relaxation, reminding him to tense and release each muscle group while seated.

After completing the sequence, Mr. Tyler checks the reflection box in the app and notes his current level of distress. It has dropped from an eight to a three. He closes the app and returns to his duties feeling more centered and ready to engage.

Key Considerations: Mr. Tyler

Mr. Tyler's interaction with the DBT Coach app reengages the prefrontal cortex at a time when stress has shifted control to the limbic system. The structured prompts reduce cognitive load, allowing him to follow guided steps even while in distress. Cold exposure activates the parasympathetic nervous system through the trigeminal nerve.[18] Movement and breathwork lower sympathetic arousal and restore balance. As each step progresses, the amygdala's activity decreases and executive functioning begins to recover, helping him shift from reactivity to regulation.[19]

CHAPTER SUMMARY

Chapter Six of *Transformational Tools for Special Educators* provides five evidence-based self-regulation techniques designed to support special education professionals in maintaining emotional balance and resilience. These tools include breathwork, cognitive reframing, grounding techniques, progressive muscle relaxation, and DBT-informed strategies. Each strategy offers a practical approach to managing stress, reducing reactivity, and promoting a sense of calm in demanding professional environments. The tools and techniques from this chapter are summarized in Table 7.1.

TABLE 7.1 Self-Regulation Tools and Techniques

TOOL	DESCRIPTION	TECHNIQUES
Breathwork	Intentional breathing techniques promote calm by focusing on the rhythm of the breath. This practice lowers stress and enhances focus.	Diaphragmatic Breathing Coherent Breathing Alternate Nostril Breathing Extended Exhalation
Cognitive Reframing	This process identifies negative thoughts, checking them for accuracy, and intentionally replacing them with alternative perspectives.	Socratic Questioning Perspective Shifting Positive Attribution Cognitive Distancing Emotional Regulation Scripts
Grounding	Grounding directs attention to external stimuli to interrupt distressing emotions. It assists with regaining emotional balance, and anchoring into the present moment	5-4-3-2-1 Grounding Objects Feet on the Floor Verbal Grounding

(Continued)

(Continued)

TOOL	DESCRIPTION	TECHNIQUES
PMR	PMR engages the body to consciously release stress. Different muscle groups are systematically tensed and released, consciously letting off stress upon release.	Classic PMR Body Scanning + PMR Autogenic Training + PMR PMR for Sleep
DBT-Informed Strategies	Selected strategies drawn from the Dialectical Behavior Therapy system that are effective in real-time when the nervous system is highly activated. These tools help disrupt reactivity, calm the body's response, and allow for executive functioning to reengage.	The STOP Method The TIPP Method

Breathwork involves intentional breathing exercises that activate your parasympathetic nervous system, reducing stress and promoting a sense of calm. Cognitive reframing focuses on identifying and challenging your negative thought patterns, replacing them with more balanced and constructive perspectives, while grounding techniques engage your senses to anchor you in the present moment, helping to reduce anxiety and prevent emotional overwhelm. Progressive Muscle Relaxation (PMR) offers a systematic method to release physical tension, which, in turn, supports your mental relaxation and well-being. Finally, DBT-informed strategies gave you two important tools that immediately interrupt intense stress in real-time, allowing you to reengage your executive functioning and proceed with clarity.

NOTES

1. Ma, X., Yue, Z. Q., Gong, Z. Q., Zhang, H., Duan, N. Y., Shi, Y. T., Wei, G. X., & Li, Y. F. (2017). The effect of diaphragmatic breathing on attention, negative affect, and stress in healthy adults. *Frontiers in Psychology, 8*, 874. https://doi.org/10.3389/fpsyg.2017.00874

2. Hamasaki, H. (2020). Effects of diaphragmatic breathing on health: A narrative review. *Medicines 7*(10), 65. https://doi.org/10.3390/medicines7100065

3. U.S. Navy Bureau of Medicine and Surgery. (n.d.). *Combat tactical breathing* [PDF]. Navy and Marine Corps Public Health Center. https://www.med.navy.mil/Portals/62/Documents/NMFA/NMCPHC/root/Documents/health-promotion-wellness/psychological-emotional-wellbeing/Combat-Tactical-Breathing.pdf.

4. Sasano, N., Vesely, A. E., Hayano, J., Sasano, H., Somogyi, R., Preiss, D., Miyasaka, K., Katsuya, H., Iscoe, S., &. Fisher, J. A. (2002). Direct effect of $paco_2$ on respiratory

sinus arrhythmia in conscious humans. *American Journal of Physiology – Heart and Circulatory Physiology,* 282(3), H973–H976. https://doi.org/10.1152/ajpheart.00554.2001

5. Lehrer, P. M., & Gevirtz, R. (2014). Heart rate variability biofeedback: How and why does it work? *Frontiers in Psychology,* 5, 756. https://doi.org/10.3389/fpsyg.2014.00756

6. Telles, S., Sharma, S. K., & Balkrishna, A. (2014). Blood pressure and heart rate variability during yoga-based alternate nostril breathing practice and breath awareness. *Medical Science Monitor Basic Research,* 20, 184–193. doi: 10.12659/MSMBR.892063

7. Goessl, R. C., Curtiss, J. E., &. Hofmann, S. G. (2017). The effect of heart rate variability biofeedback training on stress and anxiety: A meta-analysis. *Psychological Medicine,* 47(15), 2578–2586. doi: 10.1017/S0033291717001003

8. Buhle, J. T., Silvers, J. A., Wager, T. D., Lopez, R., Onyemekwu, C., Kober, H., Weber, J., Ochsner, K. N. (2014). Cognitive reappraisal of emotion: A meta-analysis of human neuroimaging studies. *Cerebral Cortex,* 24(11), 2981–2990. https://doi.org/10.1093/cercor/bht154

9. Vaish, A., Grossmann, T., & Woodward A. (20008). Not all emotions are created equal: The negativity bias in social-emotional development. *Psychological Bulletin,* 134(3), 383–403. https://doi.org/10.1037/0033-2909.134.3.383

10. Eckstein, M., Mamaev, I., Ditzen, B., & Sailer, U. (2020). Calming effects of touch in human, animal, and robotic interaction—Scientific state-of-the-art and technical advances. *Frontiers in Psychiatry,* 555058. https://doi.org/10.3389/fpsyt.2020.555058

11. Azevedo, R. T., Bennett , N., Bilicki , A., Jack Hooper, J., Fotini, M., & Manos Tsakiris, M. (2017). The calming effect of a new wearable device during the anticipation of public speech. *Scientific Reports,* 7, 2285. DOI: 10.1038/s41598-017-02274-2

12. Chellew, K., Evans, P., Fornes-Vives, J., Pérez, G., & Garcia-Banda, G. (2015). The effect of progressive muscle relaxation on daily cortisol secretion. *Stress* 18(5) 538–544. https://doi.org/10.3109/10253890.2015.1053454; Groß, D., & Kohlmann, C. W. (2021). Increasing heart rate variability through progressive muscle relaxation and breathing: A 77-day pilot study with daily ambulatory assessment. *International Journal of Environmental Research and Public Health,* 18(21), 11357. https://doi.org/10.3390/ijerph182111357; Nair B., Khan, S., Naidoo, N., Jannati, S., Shivani, B., & Banerjee, Y. (2024). Progressive muscle relaxation in pandemic times: Bolstering medical student resilience through IPRMP and Gagné's model. *Frontiers in Psychology,* 15, 1240791. https://doi.org/10.3389/fpsyg.2024.1240791

13. Jacobson, E. (1938). *Progressive relaxation.* University of Chicago Press.

14. Linehan, M. M. (1993). *Cognitive-behavioral treatment of borderline personality disorder.* Guilford Press.

15. Kinoshita, T., Nagata, S., Baba, R., Kohmoto, T., & Suketsune Iwagaki, S. (2006). Cold-water face immersion per se elicits cardiac parasympathetic activity. *Circulation Journal,* 70(6), 773–776. https://doi.org/10.1253/circj.70.773

16. Doll, A., Hölzel, B. K., Bratec, S. M., Boucard, C. C., Xie, X. Y., Wohlschläger, A. M., & Sorg, C. (2016). Mindful attention to breath regulates emotions via increased amygdala–prefrontal cortex connectivity. *NeuroImage*, *134*, 305–313. doi: 10.1016/j.neuroimage.2016.03.041

17. Craig, A. D. (2009). How do you feel—now? The anterior insula and human awareness. *Nature Reviews Neuroscience, 10*(1), 59–70. https://doi.org/10.1038/nrn2555

18. Kinoshita, T., Nagata, S., Baba, R., Kohmoto, T., & Suketsune Iwagaki, S. (2006). Cold-water face immersion per se elicits cardiac parasympathetic activity. *Circulation Journal, 70*(6), 773–776. https://doi.org/10.1253/circj.70.773

19. Doll, A., Hölzel, B. K., Bratec, S. M., Boucard, C. C., Xie, X. Y., Wohlschläger, A. M., & Sorg, C. (2016). Mindful attention to breath regulates emotions via increased amygdala–prefrontal cortex connectivity. *NeuroImage*, *134*, 305–313. doi: 10.1016/j.neuroimage.2016.03.041

CHAPTER 8

Developing Motivation

Educators are often asked to remember their "why." This *why* is the core reason they chose the field of education and is usually rooted in a desire to make a meaningful impact, inspire others, or contribute to a greater purpose. When you are connected to your purpose, you naturally access internal motivation, which gives you the energy needed to sustain you when challenges arise.

Motivation is the quiet force that propels you forward even when the path seems steep and uncertain. It influences how you pursue your goals, how much effort you put into challenges, and how quickly you recover from setbacks.

While external motivators can spark action, they are often fleeting and beyond your control. The true power of motivation always comes from within. As Daniel Goleman explained, emotional intelligence is not about chasing external validation but about nurturing an inner drive to grow, adapt, and thrive.[1] Developing this kind of motivation equips you with a powerful skill that pushes you forward and helps you flourish in the face of adversity.

While external motivation depends on outside rewards, such as recognition, monetary incentives, or praise, internal motivation stems from passion, a sense of purpose, and the satisfaction derived from mastering challenges. Research in Self-Determination Theory emphasizes that intrinsic motivation is truly the key to deeper engagement and long-term satisfaction.[2]

In the chapters that follow, we will provide tools and techniques to develop your internal motivation skills. As you master this emotional intelligence domain, you will find motivation a critical asset that aligns your actions, values, and long-term aspirations. This internal alignment results in a steady drive to pursue meaningful goals that support your highest aspirations.

WHAT MOTIVATION TOOLS DO

Motivation tools are designed to cultivate internal motivation consistently and intentionally. For example, a teacher sets a personal goal to create a classroom environment where students feel safe and valued. Instead of relying on external acknowledgement, she uses intrinsic motivation by setting a small, specific goal aligned with her larger goal: She will have at least one meaningful, positive interaction with a student every day, whether it's a genuine compliment, asking about their interests, or simply making eye contact and specifically acknowledging them. She logs her progress, and each time she meets her goal, the satisfaction triggers a natural release of dopamine that boosts her mood and reduces stress. This positive feedback loop keeps her motivated by shifting her focus from challenges to achievements, reinforcing her sense of purpose, and making her efforts feel genuinely rewarding.

Motivation plays two critical roles within the framework of this book. First, it serves as a vital skill for preventing and reducing burnout by helping individuals stay connected to personally meaningful goals. Chronic stress often emerges when individuals feel disconnected from their purpose, uncertain about their goals, or overwhelmed by challenges that appear insurmountable. Motivation tools counteract these patterns by clarifying what matters and breaking larger goals into manageable, intrinsically meaningful steps. These techniques help reduce emotional strain, making the challenges of work more manageable. Second, motivation is the driving force behind becoming the best at what you do. It is what moves people beyond merely meeting expectations and pushes them toward mastery. Motivation sustains effort, sharpens focus, and helps individuals direct their energy toward long-term goals that matter, making both well-being and excellence possible.

In high-pressure environments where external stressors can deplete energy and perseverance, motivation tools are particularly valuable. Special educators must sustain motivation despite challenges such as student disengagement, legal or administrative demands, and fluctuating emotional climates. By implementing the strategies offered in the next chapter, you can regulate your drive and maintain resilience despite any obstacles you encounter.

WHY MOTIVATION TOOLS WORK

Neurologically, the brain's reward system (particularly the mesolimbic pathway) plays a central role in reinforcing goal-directed behavior. Research shows that dopamine, a neurotransmitter associated with motivation and pleasure, is released when a person anticipates a reward.[3] This means that motivation increases in environments where positive outcomes are *expected,* and this strengthens your motivational drive. Additionally, Carol Dweck's work on Growth Mindset emphasizes the impact of belief systems on motivation.[4] Those who view challenges as opportunities for growth are more likely to sustain motivation and resilience over time.

Self-Determination Theory highlights the importance of autonomy, competence, and relatedness in creating intrinsic motivation.[5] When individuals feel a sense of control over their actions, believe in their ability to succeed, and experience social support, they are more likely to stay motivated. This theory underscores why tools such as goal-setting, feedback mechanisms, and structured accountability are so effective.

The role of neuroplasticity in motivation is also relevant. Research demonstrates that repeated engagement in goal-directed activities leads to structural changes in the brain that strengthen the neural pathways associated with persistence and effort regulation.[6]

Taken together, the studies suggest that motivation is shaped by a combination of belief systems, social and environmental factors, and neurological processes. Dopamine pathways are an important key to why motivation tools work, as they reinforce effort when rewards are both received and anticipated. Growth mindset influences how you interpret challenges moving you from a state of frustration to feeling excited about potential opportunities, and autonomy, competence, and relatedness sustain your motivation through positive feelings of mastery.

QUICK SUMMARY

Motivation is the sustaining force behind both personal resilience and professional excellence. Grounded in belief systems, strengthened through repeated effort, and reinforced by the brain's natural reward systems, motivation helps you manage stress, reduce burnout, and maintain a connection to what matters most. The next chapter explores the tools and techniques you can use to develop internal motivation. With consistent practice, you create the remarkable opportunity to thrive, excel, and ultimately become your best self both personally and professionally.

 **Reflections**

When you think about your "why" for entering the field of education:

1. How connected do you feel to it today?

_____

_____

_____

_____

_____

_____

(Continued)

(Continued)

2. What might help you connect more fully?

_____

_____

_____

_____

_____

This chapter introduced how belief systems, brain responses, and social dynamics all influence motivation.

3. Which part of this felt most familiar or most surprising to you?

_____

_____

_____

_____

_____

4. How might that insight shape what you hope to strengthen as you explore new motivation tools?

_____

_____

_____

_____

_____

NOTES

1. Goleman, D. (1995). *Emotional intelligence: Why it can matter more than IQ*. Bantam Books.

2. Deci, E. L., & Ryan, R. M. (2008). Self-determination theory: A macrotheory of human motivation, development, and health. *Canadian Psychology, 49*(3), 182–85. doi:10.1037/a0012801

3. Schultz, W. (1998). Predictive reward signal of dopamine neurons. *Journal of Neurophysiology, 80*(1), 1–27. https://doi.org/10.1152/jn.1998.80.1.1

4. Dweck, C. S. (2006). *Mindset: The new psychology of success*. Random House.

5. Deci, E. L., & Ryan, R. M. (1985). *Intrinsic motivation and self-determination in human behavior*. Plenum Press.

6. Draganski, B., Gaser, C., Busch, V., Schuierer, G., Bogdahn, U., & May, A. (2004). Changes in grey matter induced by training. *Nature 427*, 311–312. doi: 10.1038/427311a.

CHAPTER 9

Motivation Tools

Motivation is the final internal domain explored in this book, and it is a critical emotional intelligence skill. This chapter introduces three practical tools that build and strengthen this essential domain: intrinsic goal setting, self-efficacy, and mindset development (see Figure 9.1). Each of these tools offers a unique method for enhancing your ability to stay internally motivated, whether you are working toward long-term aspirations or navigating short-term challenges.

As in previous chapters, we have chosen these tools for their practical application and proven effectiveness in real-world situations. By working to increase your intrinsic (internal) motivation, you will achieve higher engagement, reduced stress, and sustained success. Regardless of which tool you choose, using it consistently is the key to success.

INTRINSIC GOAL SETTING

Tool Number One: Intrinsic Goal Setting

Have you ever felt a deep sense of purpose that seemed more important than your paycheck? Most special educators know this feeling very well. But in a profession where the challenges are high and recognition can be rare, staying connected to that inner motivation isn't always easy. Intrinsic goal setting can keep you connected to your purpose by showing you how to set goals that align with your deepest values and aspirations. When your goals connect with what truly matters to you, motivation draws you toward a path of lasting fulfillment and resilience.

Goal-setting strategies grounded in Self-Determination Theory emphasize the importance of supporting three basic psychological needs: autonomy, competence, and relatedness. Goals that align with your inherent interests and personal growth (intrinsic goals) are more likely to satisfy your needs and lead to sustained engagement and long-term persistence.[1]

FIGURE 9.1 Motivation Tools

SELECTED TOOLS FOR MOTIVATION

Intrinsic Goal Setting

Intrinsic goal setting is the process of setting goals driven by personal fulfillment, curiosity, and growth rather than external rewards, fostering lasting motivation and resilience.

Self-Efficacy

Self-efficacy is rooted in Social Cognitive Theory and works to build trust and belief in the ability to overcome challenges. This belief shapes how one handles setbacks, make decisions, and ultimately achieve one's goals.

Mindset Development

Mindset development cultivates a growth-oriented mindset where challenges become opportunities. This approach is based on Growth Mindset Theory where potential is dynamic and expands through effort and learning.

Techniques for Intrinsic Goal Setting

Values Assessment

Before setting an intrinsic goal, you must be clear about what matters most to you. Clarifying your values is crucial to setting goals that align with your personal principles, and that is the key to tapping into internal motivation.

This process can be achieved by journaling, brainstorming, or just thinking about what you are passionate about. Free online tools like the Valued Living Questionnaire (VLQ) or the Acceptance and Commitment Therapy (ACT) Values Card Sort can be extremely helpful in gaining clarity on your core values. Either tool can help you examine a range of core values to decide which ones guide your life most meaningfully.[2]

Once your values are clear, consider the ways in which you are fully living with them. You might notice that some values show up daily, while others feel neglected. This gap is important and can guide you toward a starting point when it comes to setting your intrinsic goals.

Self-Concordant Goal Setting

Once you have a clear understanding of your personal values, the next step is to set goals that align closely with those values. For example, if one of your core values in the workplace is respect, your goal might be to create a culture of respect where everyone is acknowledged for their unique perspective and inherent worth. This could be a goal for the classroom, building, or district, depending on your role or title.

After setting your goal(s), it is important to assess the source of motivation. True self-concordant goals arise from internal desires, so the assessment phase makes sure that you are focusing internally. You may ask questions like, "Why do I want to achieve this goal?" and "Would I still pursue this if there were no external rewards or recognition?" If a goal feels more like a response to external pressure, it may need to be adjusted to better align with your personal values.

Once you have evaluated the goal, it is time to create a plan to meet it. The action plan should break the goal into smaller, manageable steps. For instance, if you are an assistant principal who values respect and your goal is to create a culture of respect within your building, you may start by developing a slogan for your school like "Every Voice Matters." Additional steps might be organizing staff workshops to discuss and define respectful behaviors, setting up forums where both staff and students can share experiences of respect in action, and establishing a recognition system that celebrates everyday moments of respect. It is important that each time you accomplish a small step, you reflect on your success. This approach keeps motivation high by consistently linking actions to a deeper sense of purpose, resulting in sustained engagement and long-term fulfillment.[3]

Implementing Intrinsic Goal Setting

Ms. Thompson

Ms. Thompson, a middle school assistant principal, noticed her passion for mentoring newly hired special education teachers dwindling under the weight of administrative paperwork and urgent parent meetings. Daily tasks leave her drained of energy, and new teacher mentoring moves to the bottom of her list, as this is not one of her most urgent tasks. When a veteran teacher shares

(Continued)

(Continued)

-

-

-

-

-

Key Considerations: Ms. Thompson

By tying her mentorship goal directly to deeply held values, Ms. Thompson taps into the intrinsic rewards that originally drove her to become a principal and mentor. The process of self-concordant goal setting, followed by seamlessly integrating her goals into her existing routine, reinforces consistency without adding stress. Each time she marks a completed mentorship goal in her log, she stimulates the brain's reward circuitry, including dopaminergic pathways, which reinforces the habit of consistent follow-through.

Progress tracking provides tangible evidence of her achievements, creating a positive feedback loop that boosts motivation and maintains focus on her core values. The emphasis on linking small, daily actions to long-term aspirations fosters resilience and enhances neural networks associated with perseverance and goal-directed behavior. Over time, this alignment of everyday practices with intrinsic motivations supports neuroplastic changes that help her remain calm, focused, and dedicated, even amid high-stress administrative demands.

Technological Options for Intrinsic Goal Setting

Discovering your values and aligning your goals to those values is a personal and exploratory process. There are currently no mobile applications to assist directly with this process, but the websites mentioned earlier in this section can provide clarity on what matters most to you, and setting goals based on that knowledge is a fairly straightforward process.

SELF-EFFICACY

Tool Number Two: Self-Efficacy

What if the secret to overcoming challenges was not just about talent or knowledge but about a firm belief in your ability to succeed? Self-efficacy is a powerful perception that you are *capable* based on experience, observation, and encouragement. This belief shapes how you handle setbacks, make decisions, and ultimately achieve your goals. The strongest foundation for success lies in the trust we build in ourselves.

Self-efficacy development is rooted in Social Cognitive Theory and refers to belief in your ability to organize and carry out the actions needed to accomplish tasks and overcome challenges. According to Bandura, there are four primary sources that cultivate belief in your capability:[4]

1. *Mastery Experiences*: Successfully performing a task is the most influential way to gain a sense of efficacy.

2. *Vicarious Experiences*: Observing others who are similar to you succeed raises your beliefs that you possess the capabilities to master comparable activities.

3. *Verbal Persuasion*: Being verbally persuaded through coaching, for example, that you have the capabilities to succeed plays a role in developing your belief in self-efficacy.

4. *Physiological and Affective States*: How you interpret your physical and emotional reactions, such as anxiety, stress, or mood, influences your judgment of efficacy. Managing these states effectively supports higher self-efficacy.

Self-efficacy development directly influences perseverance, decision-making, and adaptability. Research demonstrates that individuals with high self-efficacy persist longer in difficult tasks, experience less stress, and are more likely to achieve their goals.[5]

Techniques for Self-Efficacy

Mastery Experiences

Mastery experiences are one of the most powerful ways to build self-efficacy. This technique allows you to engage in a series of progressively challenging tasks that lead to both small and larger successes. Each achievement provides concrete evidence of your competence, thus reinforcing your belief in your ability to manage future challenges effectively.

To create mastery experiences, start by breaking larger goals or tasks into smaller, manageable steps (micro-goals). Focus on setting specific, achievable goals that challenge but do not overwhelm you. As each task is completed, reflect on your accomplishment and recognize the skills and strategies that contributed to your success. This process helps build a mental record of your competence and fuels the intrinsic motivation to take on more complex tasks. For example, when learning a new skill, set micro-goals like completing a training module, applying what you learned in a real-world scenario, and evaluating the outcome of using the new skill. Celebrate your small wins to solidify your sense of progress and competence.

To further illustrate this technique, imagine that you are a teacher leader responsible for presenting weekly staff attendance data to your peers and administrators. Public speaking makes you very nervous. During your delivery, your voice sometimes cracks, and you speak at a fast pace, which prompts audience members to ask for clarification. You realize that strong presentation skills will be essential to your goal of becoming an assistant administrator, so you decide to build your skills and confidence through a series of small, achievable goals. At each step below, you celebrate your progress by acknowledging your improvements and reflecting on how far you have come.

Micro-Goals:

1. Before the next meeting, watch two to three of the most reputable tutorials on public speaking techniques, focusing on things like vocal tone, body language, and pacing. After each tutorial, write one

technique you plan to practice during the next presentation. *Finishing this small goal provides a feeling of empowerment. You are taking the first steps in developing this important skill.*

2. To help with anxiety, set a timer to quietly remind you to use focused breathwork prior to your weekly presentation to ensure that you stay grounded and regulated before speaking. *Remembering to practice breathwork before you speak brings a sense of calm to your presentation immediately, and this motivates you to grow further.*

Once you are consistently applying techniques from the tutorials and integrating breathwork each week, your next micro-goal could be to select two trusted staff members to offer feedback after your data review for the next three to four weeks. Ask them to highlight one strength in your presentation and one area for improvement each week. Commit to maintaining what works well while building your skills in areas of improvement. By knowing your strengths and focusing only on one or two areas of improvement for each presentation, you show progress each week, and this motivates your continued growth and resilience.

Visualization

Visualization involves mentally rehearsing success before it happens. When you visualize, your brain activates neural pathways that closely resemble those used during real-life experiences. For instance, if you imagine yourself attending an IEP meeting fully prepared and respected by all team members, your brain processes the scene in a way that helps you feel more familiar and confident when the situation actually occurs. Visualization builds confidence and prepares you to meet challenges with greater composure and effectiveness.

To practice effective visualization, find a quiet space and focus on a specific goal or challenge. Close your eyes and imagine yourself successfully navigating the situation. It is very important to engage all of your senses. Think about what you see, hear, and feel when navigating the situation **successfully**. Visualize the positive outcome but also the steps you take to get there. The more detailed and vivid your imagery, the stronger the impact will be on your internal motivation. Combining visualization with reflective journaling by noting the emotions and thoughts experienced during the mental rehearsal is particularly effective.

Studies suggest that visualization enhances self-efficacy by providing a mental blueprint for success. Research in performance psychology indicates that athletes, professionals, and students who use visualization techniques perform better and maintain higher motivation levels, especially in challenging situations.[6]

Self-Monitoring

Self-monitoring involves regularly assessing your progress, evaluating your strategies, and making adjustments to maintain alignment with personal goals. This technique provides a proactive approach to growth and success.

Begin by setting aside dedicated time each week for self-reflection. Use a journal or a structured template to document what went well, what challenges arose, and how they were managed. Ask specific questions like, "What strategies helped me succeed?" and "How can I apply this learning to future challenges?" Self-monitoring can also involve setting measurable goals and tracking progress through charts or logs. When setbacks occur, view them as opportunities to learn and refine your approach. This method not only builds self-efficacy but also helps maintain motivation by keeping personal growth at the forefront of your actions.

A good example of this technique is a special education teacher who engages in a structured self-monitoring script at the end of each day. Ten minutes before she leaves to go home, she addresses each question:

1. *What went well*: A group discussion sparked engagement and thoughtful responses.

2. *What challenges stand out*: A writing prompt left students confused and frustrated.

3. *What adjustment can be made*: Provide a brief example at the start of class next time, then facilitate a short, guided discussion to help students generate ideas.

Zimmerman highlighted that self-reflection and self-monitoring are key practices for enhancing self-regulated learning and self-efficacy.[7] Individuals who regularly assess their progress and adapt their strategies maintain higher levels of motivation and achieve better outcomes in personal and professional settings.

Implementing Self-Efficacy

Ms. Brown

Ms. Brown, a dedicated special education teacher, is determined to improve her classroom management skills to better support students with behavioral challenges. Instead of tackling her classroom management plan as a whole, she applies the mastery experiences approach by breaking it into a series of specific, manageable micro-goals.

She starts by identifying key areas for improvement, such as setting clear expectations, implementing effective positive reinforcement strategies, and managing transitions smoothly. She sets a focused goal for each week. In the first week, her goal is to establish a visual schedule to help students understand the daily routine. She researches best practices, creates the schedule, and introduces it to the class. She observes how students respond, makes small adjustments, and tracks her progress in a reflective journal.

After achieving this initial goal, Ms. Brown sets her sights on the next step: introducing a reward system to encourage positive behavior. She designs a simple points-based system, implements it in her classroom, and once again reflects on its effectiveness. Each week, she builds on the previous success by introducing a new technique, such as using nonverbal cues to guide behavior or setting up structured routines for transitions.

To maintain her momentum, Ms. Brown combines her mastery experiences with self-monitoring. She dedicates time every Friday to review her journal, assess what strategies worked, and refine her approach for the following week. She also creates a chart to visually track her progress toward her ultimate goal of a well-managed classroom. Whenever a strategy doesn't yield the desired results, she treats it as a learning opportunity, analyzing what adjustments might lead to better outcomes.

Through this process, Ms. Brown not only witnesses tangible improvements in classroom behavior but also experiences a boost in her self-efficacy. Each small success reinforces her belief that she can handle increasingly complex challenges. The structured approach of setting micro-goals, celebrating each achievement, and reflecting on her progress builds a strong foundation of competence and confidence. By creating a series of mastery experiences, she transforms classroom management from a daunting task into a journey of continuous growth and achievement.

Key Considerations: Ms. Brown

By systematically setting micro-goals and achieving small wins through her mastery experiences approach, Ms. Brown builds a powerful mental record of her competence. Each time she successfully implements a new classroom management strategy, her brain's reward system is activated, releasing dopamine that reinforces her belief in her abilities. This neurochemical response not only boosts her motivation but also strengthens the neural pathways associated with resilience and perseverance.

Her practice of logging successes and reflecting on what contributed to each achievement deepens this effect by creating tangible evidence of progress. This self-monitoring process enhances her self-awareness and allows her to visualize her journey of growth, which keeps her focused and driven.

Technological Options for Self-Efficacy

Coach.me is ideal for building self-efficacy through mastery experiences and intrinsic motivation. The app allows users to set and achieve incremental goals, providing personalized coaching and verbal persuasion that supports confidence and competence. The focus is on habit formation through internal growth and reflection.

Day One enhances self-efficacy through self-monitoring. By documenting daily achievements and reflecting on progress, users create a mental record of competence and success. This practice promotes intrinsic motivation by allowing individuals to recognize their growth and the strategies that contribute to it.

Trello facilitates mastery experiences by allowing users to break down larger goals into smaller, manageable tasks. Its visual project management tools support self-monitoring, helping individuals see tangible evidence of their progress. Trello enhances intrinsic motivation by emphasizing achievement through personal effort and clear visualization of completed tasks.

Implementing Self-Efficacy With Technology
Mr. Johnson

Mr. Johnson, a special education speech-language pathologist, has been directed to incorporate innovative therapy techniques into his practice, including technology-based methods that better engage his students. At first, he feels intimidated by the task. The thought of navigating new technology while maintaining effective therapy sessions is daunting, and the pressure to achieve immediate success adds to his stress.

Since he is relatively comfortable using apps, Mr. Johnson tries Coach.me. He sets small, manageable goals and breaks the larger objective (incorporating innovative technology) into specific, actionable steps. He begins with a simple goal, such as completing a training module on a new app designed to support speech therapy, then moves to more direct goals, such as implementing the new technique on one student for six sessions, comparing the student's data with and without the technology. The app's straightforward design allows him to track his progress, set daily intentions, and reflect on each success. The coaching prompts within Coach.

me provide guidance and reinforce his achievements, helping him build a tangible record of competence.

As he moves through each micro-goal, what once felt overwhelming starts to seem possible. Instead of remaining stressed and overwhelmed with the weight of the task, Mr. Johnson gains momentum. He dedicates time each week to review his progress, celebrating his successes and thoughtfully adjusting his approach when needed. This structured process shifts his perspective, and he begins to believe that he can incorporate technology and create a more engaging therapy experience for his students.

Over time, his initial sense of intimidation gives way to a growing sense of capability. Each success not only bolsters his self-efficacy but also fuels his intrinsic motivation, empowering him to integrate technology-based strategies with a sense of skill and assurance.

Key Considerations: Mr. Johnson

By leveraging Coach.me, Mr. Johnson engages in a methodical process of incremental goal-setting that activates his prefrontal cortex, strengthening the neural circuits necessary for planning and executing complex tasks. The platform's real-time feedback and measurable achievements trigger dopamine release, enhancing his confidence as he masters new therapy techniques. This consistent reinforcement transforms his initial feelings of intimidation into a growing sense of capability.

As Mr. Johnson progresses through each micro-goal, his mindset shifts from overwhelm to possibility. The structured approach helps him celebrate small victories, reflect on his progress, and make thoughtful adjustments along the way. This not only builds his self-efficacy but also boosts his intrinsic motivation, empowering him to integrate technology-based strategies into his therapy sessions with assurance and skill.

The neurobiological benefits of this approach bolster his resilience, ensuring that Mr. Johnson remains motivated and capable of adopting innovative techniques, even amidst the high demands of his professional role.

MINDSET DEVELOPMENT

Tool Number Three: Mindset Development

When learning a new task, have you ever thought, "I'm just not good at this." What if instead, you perceive each challenge as an opportunity to learn and grow? This shift from viewing your abilities as fixed to believing they can expand through effort lies at the core of mindset development. Mindset development is about cultivating a growth-oriented mindset where you view challenges as opportunities and effort as a path to mastery. This approach is based on Carol Dweck's growth mindset theory,[8] which differentiates between a fixed mindset, where you believe your abilities are static, and a growth mindset, where you understand that your potential is dynamic and can expand through effort and learning.

Developing a growth mindset within the framework of emotional intelligence enhances internal motivation by helping you stay engaged, optimistic, and persistent when facing challenges. The following are three research-backed tools that develop a growth mindset, enhancing internal motivation within the framework of emotional intelligence.

Techniques for Mindset Development

Growth Mindset Interventions

Growth mindset interventions are practical tools that guide you in transforming how you perceive your abilities and potential. Instead of viewing your intelligence and skills as fixed traits, a growth mindset encourages you to see them as qualities that can develop through effort, learning, and perseverance. This shift in perspective allows you to navigate challenges with confidence and persistence. The following are practices that cultivate a growth mindset:

- *Reframe challenges as opportunities:* When you encounter a difficult situation, consciously change your perspective. Instead of thinking, "I'm not good at this," replace that thought with, "This is an opportunity to learn and grow." This shift in thinking helps you approach challenges with curiosity and optimism. It reduces the fear of failure and encourages perseverance.

- *Set goals that focus on the process:* When setting goals, emphasize effort and learning rather than just the outcome. For example, instead of setting a goal to achieve a specific result, such as "Get a promotion," set a process-focused goal like "Improve my skills by completing a training course." This approach keeps you motivated and engaged by highlighting the progress you make through consistent effort.

- *Reflect on your experiences regularly:* After completing a task or facing a challenge, take time to reflect on what you learned and how your effort contributed to the outcome. Keeping a journal where you document your progress can help you identify the strategies that helped you overcome obstacles. This practice reinforces the connection between effort and growth and strengthens your belief in your ability to improve.

- *Learn from setbacks:* When things do not go as planned, view setbacks as valuable learning experiences. Instead of getting discouraged, analyze what went wrong, identify what you can learn from the experience, and think about how to apply those lessons moving forward. This practice builds resilience and helps you develop a proactive and adaptive approach to future challenges.

- *Engage in activities that reinforce a growth mindset:* Incorporate exercises into your routine that support a growth mindset. You might watch videos or read articles about brain plasticity, participate in workshops that focus on mindset development, or practice growth-oriented thinking in everyday situations. These activities can help you internalize the belief that your abilities can grow with effort and persistence.

Attributional Reframing

Attributional reframing is a powerful cognitive tool that involves changing how you interpret your successes and failures. Instead of attributing success to luck or fixed traits, you learn to attribute outcomes to factors within your control, such as effort, strategy, and perseverance. This approach helps build a growth mindset by reinforcing the idea that your actions and choices significantly influence your results. This approach aligns with Bernard Weiner's attribution theory,[9] which emphasizes the impact of attributions on motivation and behavior. By learning to attribute outcomes to your actions and choices, you enhance the ability to maintain motivation through challenges. The following are ways to engage in attributional reframing.

- *Identify your current attributions:* When experiencing success or failure, analyze your initial thoughts about the causes of these outcomes. Recognize if you tend to attribute success to external factors or blame failures on fixed traits. Awareness of these default attributions is the first step toward change.

- *Shift your perspective to controllable factors:* Reframe your thoughts to focus on aspects within your control. For instance, instead of thinking, "I succeeded because I was lucky," consider, "My preparation and effort led to this result." When facing setbacks, replace thoughts like "I am not good at this" with "I can improve by practicing and trying different strategies." This shift reinforces the belief that your actions directly influence outcomes.

- *Ask yourself constructive questions:* Reflect on experiences by asking questions that promote learning and improvement, such as, "What actions helped me achieve this?" or "What changes can I make to improve next time?" This method maintains focus on growth rather than perceived limitations.

- *Practice reframing in real-time:* When noticing negative or fixed-mindset thoughts, actively reframe them. For example, change "I am not talented enough" to "I can develop my skills with more practice and learning from this experience." Consistent practice helps establish positive attributions as habitual responses.

- *Reinforce the connection between effort and outcomes:* Regular reflection on how effort and strategies contribute to successes can be beneficial. Maintaining a journal of progress helps recognize patterns and keeps focus on controllable factors. Over time, this practice builds confidence and reinforces a growth-oriented mindset.

This technique can be illustrated by considering a paraprofessional who works in a self-contained classroom for students with emotional-behavioral disorders. A student refuses to follow his directions and becomes highly escalated during a group activity. Despite the paraprofessional's attempts to intervene, the student does not de-escalate, and administration has to be called for support. Example 1 illustrates the thought processes that often occur in situations like these, while Example 2 shows the power of attributional reframing:

Example 1: At the end of the day, James feels frustrated and defeated, thinking, "I'm just not cut out for this kind of work. Some people are naturally better at handling difficult behaviors, and I'm clearly not one of them." The next time a similar situation arises, James hesitates, doubting his ability to make a difference. Over time, his confidence declines, and he becomes less engaged in his role.

Example 2: At the end of the day, James feels frustrated, and he starts to question if he is a good fit for this role. He takes a moment to reframe his thoughts, considering, "This was a tough situation, but I know I can learn strategies to respond more effectively next time." He reflects on what worked and what didn't, then asks the classroom teacher for feedback. Together, they discuss alternative approaches, such as using visual cues and providing a calm space before the student becomes overwhelmed. The next time a similar situation occurs, James applies the new strategies and notices a slight improvement, as the student did not escalate to the same level as before. This motivates him to continue learning and observing so that he can build his skills and become effective in his role.

Attributional reframing engages specific brain regions associated with self-regulation, learning, and emotional processing. The prefrontal cortex becomes more active as you shift your thoughts to focus on effort and strategy, supporting decision-making and goal-setting. The hippocampus aids in integrating new strategies and learning from experiences. The anterior cingulate cortex plays a role in managing emotional responses and evaluating outcomes, helping you maintain a balanced perspective when facing setbacks. This process strengthens the connection between your efforts, strategic thinking, and achieving positive outcomes.

Process-Oriented Goal Setting

Process-oriented goal setting emphasizes your actions, habits, and the steps that lead to your goal, without worrying about the outcome. This technique is all about the journey, and not the destination. The following is an outline of the basic process:

1. Clarify your focus
2. Set specific and measurable process goals
3. Break process goals into manageable steps
4. Develop a structured plan
5. Implement and track progress
6. Reflect and adjust: Regularly review your process
7. Celebrate and iterate: Recognize and celebrate your small wins along the way

According to Locke and Latham's goal-setting theory,[10] focusing on the process rather than just the outcome enhances motivation and performance. Research demonstrates that when you adopt a process-oriented approach, you build a stronger growth mindset, exhibit greater persistence, and maintain higher levels of engagement over time.

Mental Contrasting with Implementation Intentions (MCII) is a powerful, research-backed method of process-oriented goal setting. By combining visualization with strategic planning, *Mental contrasting* strengthens motivation by vividly envisioning your desired goal and then contrasting it with potential obstacles. This creates a cognitive and emotional bridge between desire and reality. *Implementation intentions* refine this process by forming structured "if-then" plans to address obstacles proactively, and this increases the likelihood of follow-through. By combining motivation with action planning, MCII transforms the pursuit of your goals into deliberate, emotionally informed processes that support persistence and adaptive problem-solving. This method has proven successful across various contexts, including education, health, and a variety of workplace settings, supporting positive behavior change and sustained motivation.[11]

The WOOP method provides a structured, user-friendly framework that allows you to easily implement MCII. WOOP stands for Wish, Outcome, Obstacle, and Plan and is described below.

- *Wish:* Identify a specific and meaningful goal. This goal should be challenging yet attainable and aligned with personal values and long-term aspirations.

- *Outcome:* Visualize the best possible result of achieving the goal. Focus on the positive feelings and benefits that success would bring.

- *Obstacle:* Recognize potential internal and external obstacles that could hinder progress. This step involves being honest about challenges such as self-doubt, lack of time, or specific situational barriers.

- *Plan:* Create an "if-then" plan to address each obstacle. These plans are specific and actionable, providing a clear response to potential setbacks. For example, "If I start to feel overwhelmed, then I will take a five-minute break to reset."

Implementing Mindset Development

Ms. Chen

Ms. Chen, a second-year occupational therapist, felt disheartened during a session with a client who was struggling to develop fine motor control. A review of the data showed that not only was progress slow for this student, but most of her students were not making significant progress, despite her dedicated efforts. Ms. Chen felt frustrated by the lack of student improvement overall. She found herself thinking, "Maybe I'm just not good at this." Despite her passion for helping students, the challenges of her new role were starting to weigh on her confidence. Each session felt tougher than the last, and this negative self-talk crept in more frequently.

Ms. Chen chose to try attributional reframing by asking herself a powerful question: "What specific strategies could I adjust to better support my students?"

This question helped her break down challenging sessions into clear, manageable parts. For example, during the next few sessions, she discovered that her standard approach to explaining tasks wasn't working well for most students. They seemed unsure and confused when she presented a task and explained what to do. At first, she viewed this confusion as evidence of her incompetence, but she intentionally shifted her thinking and asked the question again, "What specific strategies could I adjust to better support my students?" Her answer was to view the student's confusion as a cue to try new communication techniques. The next day, Ms. Chen began to use live demonstrations and interactive discussions to clarify each step, allowing students to observe and then practice the tasks or movements before performing them. She noticed immediate results. Students were much more clear and engaged with her new approach.

Now that students were clear on what to do, Ms. Chen noticed that some of her clients became noticeably upset when they could not perform a task

Key Considerations: Ms. Chen

By reframing each challenging session as an opportunity for growth, Ms. Chen builds a powerful internal record of her competence. Each time she adjusts her communication techniques or increases her use of positive feedback and then sees even a modest improvement in her client's engagement, her brain's reward system is activated. This release of dopamine reinforces her belief in her ability to learn from setbacks, strengthening the neural pathways associated with resilience and perseverance.

By recognizing that client frustration and task refusal are natural parts of learning new skills, Ms. Chen reframes these responses as signals that more encouragement is needed rather than as signs of her inadequacy. This shift in perspective transforms setbacks into valuable learning experiences, further reinforcing her commitment to refining her strategies.

Technological Options for Mindset Development

WOOP is designed around the principles of mental contrasting and implementation intentions (MCII). It guides you through a structured process of goal visualization, obstacle identification, and if-then planning.

Implementing Mindset Development
With Technology

Mr. Carter

Mr. Carter is a special education teacher who serves students with complex learning needs. Recently, he has struggled to stay motivated, especially when trying to develop new lesson plans while juggling paperwork and frequent team meetings. He notices that he has become less engaged with his students, and he attributes this in part to the declining quality of his lesson planning due to time constraints.

To re-energize his focus, he turns to the WOOP app. Upon opening it, he is prompted to identify a *wish*, an *outcome*, an *obstacle*, and a *plan*. For Mr. Carter, the *wish* is clear: to make a positive difference for his students by helping them learn and grow. Intentional, creative lesson planning aligns closely with this core value. The app asks him to turn this into a specific, value-aligned goal, so he writes his wish: to create two creative, tailored learning modules. He selects the weekly frequency option.

When prompted to visualize and describe the *outcome*, he imagines students who are more engaged, consistently learning and progressing in measurable ways. He writes: *increased learning, engagement, and progress on IEP goals*.

Next, the app asks him to name the biggest *obstacle*. He reflects on the numerous daily demands placed on him and types: *Competing tasks*. He also recognizes that while he has a supportive administrator and an excellent paraprofessional, he often takes on too much alone.

Finally, he crafts an *if/then* plan: *If competing tasks interfere with my planning time during the week, then I will ask for support*. He adds concrete steps like asking his paraprofessional to complete daily data calculations or requesting protected planning time from his administrator.

As he tracks his progress, the app sends reminders to revisit his plan and reflect on any challenges, making adjustments as needed. Each time Mr. Carter follows through, he feels more connected to his purpose of making a meaningful impact on his students' lives.

Key Considerations: Mr. Carter

By relying on the WOOP app's structured prompts, Mr. Carter easily integrates MCII into his routine. Mentally contrasting his desired outcome with his biggest obstacle primes the anterior cingulate cortex, which becomes more adept at detecting conflicts between his overarching goal and the day-to-day demands of his job. This process allows Mr. Carter to adopt proactive solutions instead of slipping into habitual avoidance or frustration. Each successful follow-through on his if-then plan triggers continued motivation. Over time, these repeated interactions strengthen neural pathways associated with effective goal pursuit and self-regulation, ultimately making him more resilient in a high-stress environment.

This kind of technology-supported goal-setting helps Mr. Carter him stay aligned with the reasons he was drawn to special education in the first place—namely, to make a meaningful impact on his students' growth and well-being.

TIPS: Habit Stacking & Progress Tracking

Habit stacking, a term popularized by James Clear,[12] is not a direct method to implement the tools in this chapter, but it heavily supports MCII, self-concordant goal-setting, and other goal-setting techniques by providing a solid structure and the means to achieve your goals.

The power of habit stacking is powerful and impressive. Research shows that by linking a new habit to an existing routine, you significantly boost the likelihood of achieving your goals by leveraging the brain's natural "chunking" process. The progress-tracking component of this technique provides visual accountability, and this elevates motivation through dopamine release and reinforcement of adaptive feedback loops.[13]

Remember, this technique requires that you already have a clear, intrinsic goal through MCII, self-concordant goal-setting, or one that you are focused on independent of those strategies. The basic steps to this process are as follows:

1. Choose an existing habit: Pick something you already do daily, like making coffee, brushing your teeth, or sitting down at your desk.

2. Define your intrinsic goal and the related new habit: Let's say your intrinsic goal is to reduce feelings of overwhelm and start the day feeling organized and focused. This is intrinsically motivating because you want to make a real difference in the lives of your staff or students, which means you must show up as your best self. You would create an associated habit to support this goal like "Review my daily calendar " and/or "Engage in five minutes of belly breathing." Keep habits small and attainable.

(Continued)

(Continued)

3. Create your habit stack: Use this formula: "After I [existing habit], I will [new habit]." For example: "After I finish my morning coffee, I will review my calendar while belly breathing."

4. Write it down: Research shows that writing it down, whether in a journal, on a sticky note, or in a habit-tracking app, helps reinforce the habit and keeps you accountable.

5. Track your progress: Use a simple checklist, a habit tracker app, or note cards to monitor your consistency. Check off each day you complete the habit to see your progress over time.

6. Review and adjust: At the end of each week, look at your progress. If the new habit feels too easy, you can increase the challenge. If you struggle to stick to it, you can make the habit more manageable.

Habit stacking is truly one of the best ways to make your goals a reality. The challenging part of this technique is putting the initial time and thought into the small steps related to your end goal. When thoughtfully constructed, these small steps accumulate, directly supporting the realization of the goals that matter most to you.

For an example of this practice, consider the vignette for Ms. Thompson, who used the technique of self-concordant goal setting. After setting her goals, she attached them to tasks that were already a part of her workday, allowing them to build into daily habits seamlessly.

CHAPTER SUMMARY

In this chapter, we explored the critical role of motivation in emotional intelligence and professional fulfillment, offering intrinsic goal setting, self-efficacy, and growth mindset tools to sustain and enhance intrinsic motivation. A summary of these tools and techniques is provided in Table 9.1.

TABLE 9.1 Motivation Tools and Techniques

TOOL	DESCRIPTION	TECHNIQUES
Intrinsic Goal Setting	Intrinsic goal setting is the process of setting goals driven by personal fulfillment, curiosity, and growth, rather than external rewards. It fosters lasting motivation and resilience.	Value Assessment Self-concordant Goal Setting

TOOL	DESCRIPTION	TECHNIQUES
Self-Efficacy	Self-efficacy is rooted in Social Cognitive Theory and works to build trust and belief in the ability to overcome challenges. This belief shapes how one handles setbacks, makes decisions, and ultimately achieve one's goals.	Mastery Experiences Visualization Self-Monitoring
Mindset Development	Mindset development cultivates a growth-orientated mindset where challenges become opportunities. This approach is based on Growth Mindset Theory where potential is dynamic and expands through effort and learning.	Growth Mindset Interventions Attributional Reframing Process-Oriented Goal Setting emphasizing Mental Contrasting with Implementation Intentions (MCII) and the WOOP method

Intrinsic Goal Setting encourages you to discover your core values and create goals that align with those values. Self-efficacy builds confidence through mastery experiences, visualization, and self-monitoring, transforming challenges into opportunities for growth. Finally, Mindset Development encourages a growth-oriented perspective, where setbacks are reframed as learning experiences and effort is celebrated as a path to mastery. Habit stacking and progress monitoring provide a powerful structure to manifest your goals by seamlessly integrating them into your daily practice.

By integrating these tools, it becomes possible to reconnect with your "why," overcome obstacles, and achieve sustained success in your personal and professional life.

NOTES

1. Deci, E. L., & Ryan, R. M. (2000). The 'what' and 'why' of goal pursuits: Human needs and the self-determination of behavior. *Psychological Inquiry, 11*(4), 227–268. https://doi.org/10.1207/S15327965PLI1104_01

2. Murrell, J. E., & Wilson, K. G. (2004). Values Assessment and clarification as a strategy for enhancing motivation. In J. T. Blackledge & F. W. Bond (Eds.), *Acceptance and commitment therapy: Contemporary theory, research, and practice* (pp. 65–88). New Harbinger.; Miller, W. R., & Rollnick, S. (2012). *Motivational interviewing: Helping people change* (3rd ed.). Guilford Press.

3. Sheldon, K. M., & Elliot, A. J. (1999). Goal striving, need satisfaction, and longitudinal well-being: The self-concordance model. *Journal of Personality and Social Psychology, 76*(3), 482–97. doi: 10.1037//0022-3514.76.3.482

4. Bandura, A. (1997). *Self-efficacy: The exercise of control.* W. H. Freeman.

5. Bandura, A. (1997). *Self-efficacy: The exercise of control*. W. H. Freeman

6. Taylor, S. E., Pham, L. K., Rivkin, I. D., & Armor, D. A. (1998). Harnessing the Imagination: Mental simulation, self-regulation, and coping. *American Psychologist, 53*(4), 429–39. doi: 10.1037//0003-066x.53.4.429

7. Zimmerman, B. J. (2000). Self-efficacy: An essential motive to learn. *Contemporary Educational Psychology, 25*(1), 82–91. https://doi.org/10.1006/ceps.1999.1016

8. Dweck, C. S. (2006). *Mindset: The new psychology of success*. Random House.

9. Weiner, B. (1985). An attributional theory of motivation and emotion. *Psychological Review, 92*(4), 548–73. https://doi.org/10.1037/0033-295X.92.4.548

10. Locke, E. A., & Gary P. Latham, G. P. (2002). Building a practically useful theory of goal setting and task motivation: A 35-year odyssey. *American Psychologist, 57*(9), 705–17. doi: 10.1037//0003-066x.57.9.705

11. Oettingen, G. (2014). *Rethinking positive thinking: Inside the new science of motivation*. Penguin; Duckworth, A. L., Grant, H., Loew, B., Oettingen, G., & Gollwitzer, P. M. Self-regulation strategies improve self-discipline in adolescents: Benefits of mental contrasting and implementation intentions. *Educational Psychology, 31*(1), 17–26. https://doi.org/10.1080/01443410.2010.506003

12. Clear, J. (2018). *Atomic habits: An easy and proven way to build good habits and break bad ones*. Avery.

13. Oettingen, G. (2014). *Rethinking positive thinking: Inside the new science of motivation*. Penguin; Duckworth, A. L., Grant, H., Loew, B., Oettingen, G., & Gollwitzer, P. M. Self-regulation strategies improve self-discipline in adolescents: Benefits of mental contrasting and implementation intentions. *Educational Psychology, 31*(1), 17–26. https://doi.org/10.1080/01443410.2010.506003

CHAPTER 10

Applied Harmony

When you commit to developing any of the internal emotional intelligence domains (self-awareness, self-regulation, or motivation), the beginning stages of transformative change become noticeable. You may feel more centered and composed, more aware of your thoughts and feelings, or more motivated in various aspects of your work. But if you wish to deepen or accelerate your growth, combining the internal tools into your daily practice can take your skills to a higher level. The result is a more integrated version of yourself that responds to challenges with clarity, leads with intention, and sustains emotional balance even in the most demanding environments.

The internal domains work in harmony, each reinforcing the others in a balanced, purposeful way. When used together, these tools create a powerful process of reflection and meaningful action. Self-awareness provides the foundation for recognizing emotions and identifying thought patterns, and self-regulation ensures that those insights translate into intentional, adaptive responses. Internal motivation supports this process by fueling the ongoing drive for growth and resilience. This chapter builds on the strategies previously discussed and provides real-world examples that combine the three internal domains of emotional intelligence for maximum impact.

Consider an educator who feels extremely frustrated during the numerous classroom disruptions throughout her day. A self-awareness tool such as reflective journaling is a great starting point, as this allows her to process the situation and identify specific emotions and their triggers. She will begin to recognize what she is feeling and what factors in the environment cause her feelings. But if she stops there, not much will change in her day-to-day experience. But if she pairs reflective journaling with box breathing during classroom disruptions, she immediately decreases the intense emotions she has identified. If she then creates an intentional plan like using positive behavior supports to reward her class when they remain calm (which aligns with her personal goal of *ensuring that all students and staff feel safe and supported in her classroom*), she creates the ability to remain calm and focused during disruptions, knowing that she is actively engaged in a purpose-driven plan to reduce these disruptions over the long term. Figure 10.1 illustrates this dynamic.

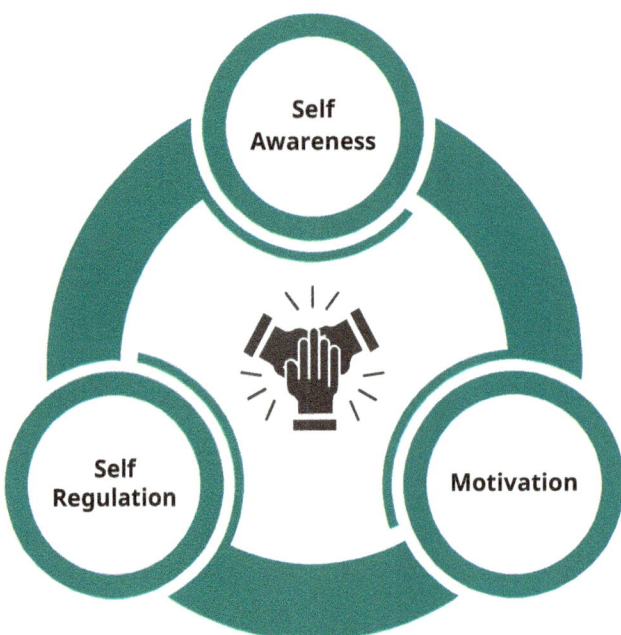

FIGURE 10.1 Harmonizing Internal Emotional Intelligence

Recognizing an emotional reaction is a critical first step, but without strategies to channel that energy, awareness alone can become overwhelming or lead to inaction. Moving from awareness to action through self-regulation tools will increase your ability to avoid burnout by reducing stress, but regulation without motivation can lack purpose and direction. Motivation practices keep you connected with what matters while focusing on your strengths and accomplishments.

The key to successful integration of internal domains is selecting tools that complement one another and create internal harmony within your daily routines. From there, your tools can be easily accessed and applied in challenging circumstances. In the following section, we will explore practical ways to combine self-awareness, self-regulation, and internal motivation techniques into your typical workday, illustrating how you can create a personalized approach that fosters emotional resilience, reduces burnout, and enhances your effectiveness.

DAILY HARMONIZING

Most self-awareness and self-regulation tools pair seamlessly because they create a natural flow from awareness to action. Instead of simply recognizing emotions, these combinations ensure that awareness translates into action. Adding motivation tools gives direction and purpose to your efforts.

Used together, these tools keep you engaged in the process of noticing, responding, and adjusting.

The techniques you have studied across self-awareness, self-regulation, and motivation are not meant to sit in theory. The following examples reveal just how naturally the tools can blend into your daily routines. Whether you use them at the start of your day, as a midday reset, or as a response to sudden stress, each combination fits effortlessly into your daily flow with no need to carve out extra time. The wonderful thing about transformative tools is that they are not time-consuming, but remember, consistency is key. The more you use these tools and techniques, the more your brain rewires to form adaptive feedback loops until staying calm under pressure, thinking clearly in the moment, and reconnecting with your purpose feels less like effort and more like instinct.

Examples of Harmonizing in Daily Practice

Amy: Proactive Balance

Amy is a special education teacher who begins her day with five to ten minutes of gratitude journaling. She writes down several specific things she is thankful for to shift her attention toward a positive emotional state. She follows this with three minutes of belly breathing to support regulation and prepare for student arrival.

Mornings are typically very busy and demanding, so at lunchtime, Amy uses body scanning and affect labeling to determine her current emotional state. If she notices emotions that need attention, she opens a guided breathing app and follows a seven-minute calming sequence before returning to class, using her HRV device to ensure that she is emotionally ready to continue the day.

Before leaving for the day, Amy spends ten minutes with her reflective journal to complete a self-monitoring practice. She answers structured questions about what went well, what challenges arose, and how she plans to adjust her strategies tomorrow if needed.

Amy's Tools and Techniques

Self-Awareness (Gratitude Practices, Body Scanning), Self-Regulation (Breathwork with and without technology), Motivation (Self-Monitoring).

Time: Less than thirty minutes total

Impact: Emotional balance and clarity, reduced reactivity, and alignment with professional aspirations

Demetrius: Setting Up for Success

Demetrius is a special education administrator who comes to work a little early so that he can begin his day with ten minutes of mindful walking before entering the building. He focuses on the rhythm of his movement and breath as he walks the school grounds, allowing the walk to calm his thoughts and bring clarity before the school day begins. If he has had a particularly stressful morning, Demetrius may incorporate mindful observation by noticing details of the ground, his shoes, or the way the light filters through the trees. He enters the building centered and ready for the day.

When Demetrius gets a break for lunch, he has usually juggled numerous tasks that require follow-up, so he uses the feet-on-the-floor technique to ground himself. He brings awareness to the contact between his feet and the floor and uses this moment to reset. If needed, he uses a PMR app and takes five minutes to release tension so that he does not carry it through the afternoon.

After school, Demetrius engages in a mastery experience by working toward a larger goal through a series of micro-goals. He is building confidence in leading small group meetings with paraprofessionals, so each day, he completes one manageable micro goal that supports his long-term plan.

These practices support Demetrius's emotional regulation, sustain his focus, and keep him motivated and connected to his leadership role.

Demetrius's Tools and Techniques

Self-Awareness (Mindfulness), Self-Regulation (Grounding, PMR), Motivation (Self-Efficacy)

Time: Fifteen minutes total for self-awareness and self-regulation. Motivation practice may vary depending on the complexity of the micro-goal.

Impact: Emotional regulation throughout the day, clear focus, and sustained motivation that promotes resilience

Marisa: Composure Under Pressure

Marisa is a special education supervisor who regularly participates in complex and (often) litigious IEP meetings. Before each meeting, she sets aside five minutes to use a guided mindfulness/breathwork script via her Insight Timer app. She follows a recording that centers her attention on breath and body awareness, gradually shifting her focus toward steady presence and composure. This helps lower the tension that most team members experience prior to high-stakes meetings.

After this exercise, she uses a two-minute visualization to rehearse the meeting in her mind. She sees herself responding to tense moments objectively by providing references to data, redirecting emotionally charged comments with ease, and maintaining a neutral, professional tone. She visualizes herself holding her role with steadiness and purpose.

During the meeting itself, if a parent or team member makes a negative or accusatory remark, Marisa applies Socratic questioning internally, jotting responses on her notepad. Instead of reacting immediately, she pauses and silently challenges the automatic interpretation. Is this personal? Is it entirely true? Is there another way to view what was just said? This pause creates space between the comment and her response, allowing her to stay grounded and respond accurately and constructively.

Marisa's Tools and Techniques

Self-Awareness (Mindfulness), Self-Regulation (Breathwork, Cognitive Reframing), Motivation (Self-Efficacy)

Time: Seven minutes before a meeting

Impact: Maintains clarity and composure under tremendous pressure

Trina: Data-Driven Mastery

Trina is a seasoned special education teacher who works with students who have emotional behavior disorders. When confronted with verbal threats or physical aggression, she immediately uses box breathing to remain steady. She inhales, holds, exhales, and pauses in equal counts, using the structure of the breath to interrupt her stress response and maintain control in the moment.

After dismissal, she spends ten minutes with her reflective journal to document select episodes, applying the cause-and-effect technique. She outlines what triggered the student, what emotion surfaced in her, and what her response contributed to the direction of the interaction. This process helps her identify patterns and emotional cues that might otherwise go unnoticed. She then applies growth mindset interventions by reframing difficult interactions as opportunities to strengthen her skills. Instead of interpreting the challenge as a sign of personal limitation, she identifies what the experience can teach her and what effort and adjustment can contribute to future improvement. She spends ten minutes setting process-focused goals, such as refining her de-escalation language or preparing more explicit regulation supports in advance.

Trina's Tools and Techniques

Self-Regulation (Breathwork), Self-Awareness (Reflective Journaling), Motivation (Mindset Development)

Time: Twenty minutes for reflective journaling and goal setting, and three minutes or less for box breathing during aggressive episodes

Impact: Maintains composure in challenging situations, finds deeper understanding of student triggers and behaviors, proactive approach to challenges, and views challenges as opportunities for growth

SITUATIONAL HARMONIZING

In moments of high stress, complex decision-making, or emotional disruption, it becomes essential to draw from a set of tools that work together with precision. The ability to respond effectively in these moments depends on frequent and regular use of emotional intelligence tools and techniques so that they are familiar, accessible, and second nature when needed most. That is why practice through daily application is crucial. In the middle of a difficult moment, there is no time to stop and recall steps from memory. These tools must already live in you through daily practice, making them familiar enough to access without hesitation and steady enough to carry you through without effort.

Situational harmonizing involves selecting tools that naturally reinforce one another. These combinations help you stay grounded when tension rises and regulate internal states when emotions escalate. This section illustrates how to combine specific self-awareness, self-regulation, and internal motivation techniques to create targeted responses that promote clarity, composure, and intentional action.

The following examples are meant to guide your thinking as you identify combinations that support your role and reflect your personal approach.

These are not formulas to follow but illustrations of how harmony among internal tools creates strength and stability in real-time. Each example represents a practical application of the techniques you have already studied and hopefully practiced in a way that fits the pace and complexity of professional life in special education.

Example One: De-escalate With Intention

Body Scanning and Box Breathing

Scenario: A school administrator is engaged in a challenging interaction with a student demonstrating aggression and making threats.

The administrator feels a familiar heat rise in her chest and a clenching in her jaw. She shifts her attention inward and scans her body, noticing that her shoulders are tight, her stomach is upset, and her hands are beginning to curl. She recognizes these early signals of anxiety and tension and consciously brings focus to her breathwork technique. She quietly engages in box breathing while continuing to scan her body. After two cycles of box breathing, she feels her posture shift. Her jaw softens, her stomach settles, and her hands relax. No longer matching the student's intensity, she can effectively utilize de-escalation strategies with the student while modeling self-regulation.

These techniques pair well because they are both used in real-time to alleviate stress and relax quickly. Body scanning brings awareness of where tension or discomfort lands in your body, and through that awareness, you can intentionally address stress by immediately using breathwork to bring about a state of calm. This powerful combination allows you to interrupt escalating physiological responses before they gain momentum, creating the internal conditions needed for clear thinking and steady action.

Example Two: A Balanced Response

Expressive Writing, Perspective Shifting, and WOOP

Scenario: A paraprofessional receives challenging feedback from her supervisor about her approach to supporting students.

The paraprofessional leaves the encounter very upset. Her first reaction is to complain to her colleagues, but she knows this will not necessarily resolve anything because, in the past, this kind of venting only escalated her feelings. During her break, she uses affect labeling to pinpoint and name exactly how she feels, then she engages in expressive writing. She feels angry and hurt by the interaction, and as she writes and externalizes the emotional impact of the critique, she begins to use perspective shifting to reinterpret the feedback. She realizes that from the administrator's perspective, her approach could seem rigid and cold because she is probably unaware that using a "neutral tone and approach" is part of many students' behavior intervention plans. The administrator is new to special education, and she may genuinely lack knowledge of the research behind the approach. She further realizes that the real issue was not about her. The administrator was clearly concerned about students, and this is where they had common ground.

The emotional release settles the paraprofessional, and now, with a clearer understanding of the encounter, she uses the WOOP app on her phone to set a goal to provide the administrator with a deeper understanding of her methodology. She assessed one obstacle as the administrator's resistance to receiving new information because of her full schedule and the learning curve in her new role as administrator to students with special needs. She decided that if resistance happens, she will remain persistent because helping the administrator understand the population she serves will benefit all students and special education staff members. This goal resonates deeply, and her motivation rises.

These tools and techniques combine to create a synergistic sequence that identifies emotional impact, shifts perception, and creates purposeful next steps. Expressive writing creates an internal pause by transforming raw emotion into narrative form, helping regulate emotional intensity through structured reflection. Perspective shifting challenges the initial interpretations of those emotions, making space for alternative viewpoints and a more nuanced understanding. After processing the emotion and expanding perspective, the WOOP method uses that insight to create forward momentum by identifying a meaningful Wish, clarifying the desired Outcome, anticipating internal Obstacles, and planning a clear Path to overcome them.

Example Three: Handling Parent Confrontations

Reflective Journaling (Selected Columns), Emotional Regulation Script, and Attributional Reframing

Scenario: A speech-language pathologist is confronted by a parent during a meeting. The parent stated sharply, "We do not see any progress. What have you actually been doing for my child?"

The therapist felt her heart rate spike. She could feel her body bracing. She paused before answering and turned to the internal script she uses in moments like these:

1. I notice tightness in my chest and a pit in my stomach. That is my body responding to what feels like a threat.

2. This feeling makes sense. It is valid to feel this way when my work is being questioned. I care deeply about what I do, and this kind of challenge matters to me.

3. I do not need to react from this place. I can take a breath and stay grounded.

With the internal pressure named and validated, she takes a breath and remains composed. She acknowledges the parent's concern and restates the child's gains with calm clarity. She stays steady throughout the rest of the meeting. Later, in her office, she sat for a moment, disappointed that the meeting did not go as planned. The parent's words stayed with her, and self-doubt crept in. She thought, "Maybe I haven't done enough."

She opens her reflective journal and begins completing the selected columns, using attributional reframing for column three:

1. **What Went Well:** I stayed grounded in the moment. I used my emotional regulation script and did not react defensively. I presented the data calmly.

2. **What Went Wrong:** I allowed the parent's words to echo after the meeting. I felt doubt creep in and did not separate their fear from my abilities and objective facts.

3. **What Can Be Learned:** The parent's comments were not objective evaluations of my competence because the data shows obvious growth. The parent may measure progress in ways that do not reflect how language development actually unfolds. The parent's frustration is not personal, even if it felt that way in the moment. I responded in a measured way, consistent with sound clinical practice. I can hold his disappointment without internalizing blame. I can use this as a prompt to clarify expectations and communication going forward.

She packed her materials and left the building without carrying negative feelings and thoughts from the encounter. The script had steadied her. The reframe had restored her motivation.

These tools work together to support emotional clarity, cognitive accuracy, and professional resilience. Emotional regulation scripts offer a structured way to recognize and validate internal states in the moment, helping maintain composure under pressure. Reflective journaling provides space to examine the encounter with intention and use attributional reframing to shift meaning, correct distortion, and extract insight. Together, they foster grounded self-awareness and a forward-facing stance rooted in professional integrity.

Example Four: Leadership Lessons
Mindful Breathing, 5-4-3-2-1, and Growth Mindset Interventions

Scenario: A lead teacher for students with special needs is new to her role but has ten years of teaching experience. One of the veteran teachers she supervises consistently responds to her directives by rolling her eyes and using a dismissive tone in response. This response occurred again when the lead teacher shared the new process for reporting students' current functioning.

The lead teacher felt her heartbeat and thoughts race. Her palms began to sweat, and her temper rose. Instead of reacting, she turned inward and practiced mindful breathing. She focused on the steady rhythm of air moving in and out of her nose. With each breath, her nervous system began to regulate, and her composure returned. Calmer now, she asked the teacher to retrieve her IEP binder so she could illustrate the new process more clearly. The teacher responded with yet another eye roll and muttered, "Sure. Whatever you say."

As the veteran teacher walked away, the lead teacher could feel her temper rising again. This time, she shifted into a sensory grounding technique: 5-4-3-2-1. She began silently identifying five things she could see—the corner of her task box, a loose thread on the mat, an open Velcro strip on the wall, a blue pen in her hand, and a crack in the ceiling tile. Next, she touched four objects: her slacks, her desk, a stress ball, and the spiraled edge of her notebook. She then named three sounds she could hear. After that, two things she could smell, and finally, one taste. As she completed the sequence, she felt a growing sense of clarity and composure.

Once grounded, she engaged in a growth mindset reflection by asking herself, "What can I learn from this situation?" The answer came quickly: Leadership requires setting clear expectations and addressing staff behavior—ideally before issues escalate. She remembered that this teacher's negativity was a common concern among her peers.

Rather than avoiding the issue, she saw this as an opportunity to grow in her leadership. Her next step would be to consult with her supervisor and the building administrator for guidance on how to proceed with setting expectations and giving professional feedback to the teacher. From there, she would map out a plan and stay accountable to her goals by checking in with herself and her mentors, especially if things did not go as planned.

By the time the teacher returned, the lead teacher felt grounded and optimistic. She handled the conversation with calm confidence, aware that she was already taking meaningful steps to support her development and leadership journey.

Mindful breathing, the 5-4-3-2-1 technique, and growth mindset interventions form a powerful triad for stabilizing emotional states and reinforcing personal growth in challenging professional moments.

Mindful breathing helps interrupt the automatic stress response by anchoring awareness in the present and allowing space between stimulus and reaction. The 5-4-3-2-1 grounding strategy deepens this presence by engaging the senses and promoting cognitive clarity when emotions threaten to cloud judgment. Growth mindset practices encourage reflection and a willingness to view setbacks as opportunities for learning and growth. They shift focus from perceived failure to the potential for development through effort and adaptability.

When used together, these tools foster composure, clarity, and a grounded mindset that supports resilience and professional integrity

Example Five: The Heart of the Matter
Affect Labeling, STOP, and Process-Oriented Goal Setting

Scenario: A special education teacher gives the class a directive to take out science books and turn to chapter 5. One of her students with a complex history of trauma takes out the book, throws it onto the floor, and begins taunting her, using profanity and personal insults.

The teacher feels her cheeks flush, and her thoughts begin to race. She grounds herself by silently naming her emotions through affect labeling. She acknowledges, "I feel disrespected. I feel cornered. I feel like I am being personally attacked." The

(Continued)

(Continued)

1.

2.

3.

4.

Affect labeling, STOP, and process-oriented goal setting work together to regulate intense emotional responses and create a constructive path forward. Affect labeling initiates cognitive control by converting raw emotion into language and reducing activation in the amygdala. The STOP technique builds on this pause by offering a structured sequence that interrupts reactive behavior and restores calm presence. Process-oriented goal setting allows the professional to integrate insight from the experience and take proactive steps that align with values and long-term support strategies. When practiced together, these tools stabilize the moment and transform disruption into purpose.

QUICK SUMMARY

Internal tools create notable changes in your balance and resilience when used in isolation. But the greatest benefit by far comes from intentionally combining them in daily practice and during challenging circumstances. By using thoughtful combinations of internal tools and techniques, you create a sense of internal harmony that supports your best work.

In the next chapter, we will shift focus from internal practices to external development. You will explore tools and techniques that strengthen connections with others, improve communication, and build collaborative relationships that support both students and teams.

Reflections

Think about the five daily harmonizing examples (Amy, Demetrius, Marisa, Trina, and Nicole).

1. Which professional's approach most closely aligns with your current role and daily routine?

_____

_____

_____

_____

_____

_____

(Continued)

(Continued)

2.

3.

4.

CHAPTER 11

External Emotional Intelligence Tools

Imagine a classroom where every interaction, whether with a student, colleague, or parent, leaves others feeling heard, valued, and motivated. This isn't just an idealistic vision; it's the result of mastering the external domains of emotional intelligence.

As noted in the beginning chapters of this book, the success of external emotional intelligence skills depends on a solid foundation of internal skills. For example, the external technique of active listening falls flat if you're too overwhelmed to stay present and engaged in conversation. Similarly, conflict resolution tools falter if emotional reactions override your problem-solving abilities. In every case, the strength of your internal tools determines the success of your external strategies.

Neurologically, every interaction with others is an opportunity to rewire your brain for better communication and resilience. Just as breathwork and affect labeling train your nervous system to engage in cognition and relax, practicing external tools like nonviolent communication or structured relationship-building strengthens neural pathways for patience, connection, and adaptability. Over time, these deliberate efforts become automatic responses, equipping you with the remarkable skill to navigate high-stress interactions with composure and grace.

External emotional intelligence domains fall into two categories:

1. *Empathy-Based Tools:* Strategies that enhance understanding of others' emotions, such as active listening, perspective-taking, and nonviolent communication.

2. *Social Skills Tools:* Skills that strengthen communication and collaboration, including conflict resolution, relationship-building, and social awareness.

WHAT EXTERNAL EMOTIONAL INTELLIGENCE TOOLS DO

Mastery of external emotional intelligence domains makes all the difference in successfully navigating professional and personal relationships. Whether in an emotionally charged environment, a collaborative planning meeting, or working one-on-one with staff, students, or parents, the tools in chapters 11 and 12 give you the power to shift the energy and shape your surroundings for the better.

When you use external tools with intention, they allow you to respond thoughtfully rather than react impulsively. For example, imagine a parent entering your classroom or school building, visibly agitated. When you approach, she sharply states, "Jim told me that you threatened and yelled at him yesterday in the lunchroom, and this is unacceptable!" A reactive response might be to immediately deny or defend your actions, or you might dismiss the parent's concern, because it is clear that her child purposefully gave her the wrong information.

Reactive responses will typically escalate any situation. In the example above, reactivity and defensiveness are sure to leave the parent feeling angry and unheard, which could motivate her to speak to the principal, tell her story on social media, or even contact the school board. What could have been a productive conversation becomes an ongoing conflict, and the student suffers when adults cannot work together.

In contrast, using an empathy-based tool like active listening can quickly shift the tone. With active listening, you pause, make direct eye contact, and reflect the emotion you observe: "It sounds like you're frustrated about what happened yesterday. I want to make sure I fully understand." This small but intentional response begins to regulate the parent's nervous system and opens the door to connection. Once that foundation is in place, a social skills tool like collaborative dialogue can move the conversation forward. With a steady tone, you might say, "Let's talk through what happened yesterday. Please explain your understanding of the encounter." This approach makes the parent feel that you care about what she has to say, and this will open her receptivity when you explain the situation from your perspective.

To further illustrate the power of using external emotional intelligence tools, imagine that you are the assistant director for special education in your school district. During a leadership team meeting, a special education supervisor speaks up abruptly, saying, "You made this decision without input from the leadership team. That's not how collaboration works." Initially, you feel a strong urge to defend your decision or clarify the process. If you choose to use Nonviolent Communication (NVC) instead, you would respond by saying, "It sounds like you're frustrated and felt left out of the process." You then tap into the underlying need: "It seems like being included in decisions that affect your team is really important to you." Finally (in accordance with the NCV tool), you offer: "Would it help if we talked through how we can collaborate more closely moving forward?" With the emotional tone addressed, you can use an effective communication tool and shift your communication style to match the collaborative setting. You might say, "Let's look at the rollout plan together and make sure it works for everyone." This brief but deliberate choice strengthens trust and models professional responsiveness.

Identical to internal tools, external tools are most effective when practiced consistently. Over time, they become second nature and guide the emotional tone of your environment, influencing how others perceive your presence and respond to your cues. Professionals who master these tools often become steadying forces in their organizations. Their interactions build trust and mutual respect, reducing the likelihood of escalation and increasing the chances of productive outcomes.

WHY EXTERNAL EMOTIONAL INTELLIGENCE TOOLS WORK

Empathy-based tools, including perspective-taking, emotional validation, and reflective listening, engage the medial prefrontal cortex, which is the same region involved in self-awareness.[1] This region plays a critical role in integrating emotional and social data, helping you perceive what others are feeling without becoming overwhelmed by it.

Regions of your brain activate when certain external tools are used. For example, your temporoparietal junction plays a central role in the external skill of perspective-taking. It distinguishes your thoughts from someone else's, which helps you understand what another person might be feeling or intending. Interpretations of body language, vocal tone, and facial expressions are supported by the superior temporal sulcus. This region of the brain helps you read nonverbal cues and emotional shifts accurately and in real-time. Strengthening these areas of the brain enables you to respond with empathy and attunement rather than assumption or misinterpretation.[2]

Social skill tools engage areas of the brain associated with executive functioning, including the dorsolateral prefrontal cortex and anterior cingulate cortex.[3] These regions support goal-oriented behavior, cognitive flexibility, and the inhibition of reactive impulses. When resolving a disagreement, for example, these areas of the brain allow you to weigh competing perspectives, suppress defensive reactions, and shift toward collaborative problem-solving.[4] Each time you use a social skills tool in real-time, you strengthen the neural pathways that support regulation, adaptability, and strategic communication.

External tools also trigger physiological changes that support relational stability. Active listening and emotional validation often result in the release of oxytocin, a hormone associated with trust and bonding.[5] This neurochemical shift reinforces connection and decreases the brain's threat response, creating an atmosphere where productive dialogue becomes possible. Repeated use of these tools contributes to emotional safety across settings, which is essential for both learning and collaboration. As your brain adapts to using empathy and social skills over time, your ability to maintain connection under stress becomes automatic.

QUICK SUMMARY

External emotional intelligence tools translate your internal work into outward impact. They provide structure for how you listen, respond, and relate, especially under pressure. These tools are not just useful; they are transformative. They reshape neural pathways, regulate physiological responses, and shift your interactions from reactivity to collaboration.

When practiced consistently, external tools allow you to remain grounded in yourself while making space for others. They make it possible to manage complex relationships without sacrificing authenticity or composure. Professionals who master these emotional intelligence domains create environments where everyone feels connected, respected, and empowered.

Chapter 11 provides research-based tools and techniques to develop empathy, and chapter 12 brings together the most effective tools and techniques for social skills development. Together, these chapters give you the tools to turn everyday interactions into opportunities for connection and growth.

Whether you're calming tension, building trust, or guiding a tough conversation, you'll find strategies that help you create stronger relationships in the moments that matter most.

Reflections

Think about a recent challenging interaction you had with a colleague, student, or parent.

1. How did your internal emotional state (stress level, self-awareness, emotional regulation) influence your ability to use external tools like active listening or empathy?

_____

_____

_____

_____

_____

_____

2. What would have happened differently if your internal foundation had been stronger?

_____

_____

_____

_____

_____

_____

Identify a recurring situation in your professional life where you tend to react defensively or impulsively.

3. What specific external emotional intelligence tool from this chapter could you practice in that scenario?

_____

_____

_____

_____

_____

4. How might using this tool change both the immediate outcome and the long-term relationship?

_____

_____

_____

_____

_____

NOTES

1. Decety, J., & Jackson, P. L. (2004). The functional architecture of human empathy. *Behavioral and Cognitive Neuroscience Reviews, 3*(2), 71–100. https://doi.org/10.1177/1534582304267187

2. Saxe, R., & Kanwisher, N. (2003). People thinking about thinking people: The role of the temporo-parietal junction in 'Theory of Mind.' *NeuroImage, 19(*4), 1835–42. https://doi.org/10.1016/S1053-8119(03)00230-1; Allison, T., Puce, A., & McCarthy, G. (2000). Social perception from visual cues: Role of the STS region. *Trends in Cognitive Sciences, 4*(7), 267–78. doi: 10.1016/S1364-6613(00)01501-1

3. Miller, E. K., & Cohen, J. D. (2001). An integrative theory of prefrontal cortex function. *Annual Review of Neuroscience, 24,*167–202. https://doi.org/10.1146/annurev.neuro.24.1.167

4. Gross, J. J. (2002). Emotion regulation: Affective, cognitive, and social consequences. *Psychophysiology, 39*(3), 281–91. https://doi.org/10.1017/S0048577201393198

5. Uvnäs-Moberg, K. (1998). Oxytocin May Mediate the Benefits of Positive Social Interaction and Emotions. *Psychoneuroendocrinology, 23(*8), 819–35. https://doi.org/10.1016/S0306-4530(98)00056-0

CHAPTER 12

Empathy Tools

The concept of empathy began gaining popularity in leadership, education, marketing, and social justice about fifteen years ago. Today, empathy is a widely recognizable term, reflecting its broad acceptance across most professions and its use in everyday conversations.[1]

Most people understand empathy as the ability to comprehend and share the feelings of another person, and while this is true, empathy is more than just a concept. When practiced intentionally, it is a neurological process that strengthens the brain's capacity for emotional attunement, perspective-taking, and meaningful connection.[2] In a special education setting, empathy is essential for fostering trust, de-escalating conflict, and creating an environment where individuals feel heard and valued.

Your brain has a remarkable ability to adapt to repeated behaviors, and empathy is no exception. When you engage in empathetic practices, you activate areas in your brain responsible for emotional regulation, social cognition, and connection by reinforcing neural pathways in the prefrontal cortex and mirror neuron system.[3] Over time, practicing empathy as an intentional tool rewires these neural networks, making compassionate responses more natural and automatic in high-stress situations.

Some educators are naturally empathetic, and some find this skill exceptionally challenging and in conflict with their typical communication approach. In either case, the same tools can be used to strengthen neural pathways related to empathic understanding and expression. The difference will come in the amount of consistent practice required to effectively rewire the brain, as this will vary depending on your starting point. We will explore four research-based techniques to develop this important skill as outlined in Figure 12.1. If empathy does not come naturally to you, a more deliberate, sustained use of the tools will yield the best results.

FIGURE 12.1 Selected Tools for Empathy Development

SELECTED TOOLS FOR EMPATHY DEVELOPMENT

Active Listening

Active listening fosters communication where the listener is fully present and does not offer immediate solutions. The listener reflects the speaker's comments, acknowledging emotions and asking clarifying questions to deepen understanding.

Perspecive–Taking Exercises

Perspective-taking engages the brain's mirror neurons and promotes cognitive flexibility, allowing listeners to avoid assumptions and respond with greater understanding.

Nonviolent Communication

Nonviolent Communication (NVC) emphasizes expressing feelings without judgment. It encourages empathetic listening and honest expression and is used in a variety of settings to foster productive communication.

Trauma-Informed Empathy

Trauma-informed empathy views behavior as communication. This tool increases empathy and effective interventions because challenging behavior is understood as a response to traumatic events.

ACTIVE LISTENING

Tool Number One: Active Listening

Have you ever been in conversation with a friend or colleague, and the listener was looking at her phone, gazing around the room, or just barely listening, waiting for her turn to speak? She might even interrupt you, believing she already understands what you are trying to say, even though you still have vital information to share. Active listening requires you to be fully present when listening. It is one of the most powerful ways to build empathy.[4]

By remaining present and engaged, you gain a deeper understanding of the other person's emotions, concerns, and underlying needs. Instead of offering immediate solutions or becoming defensive, active listening involves reflecting what you hear back to the speaker, acknowledging emotions, and asking clarifying questions to ensure accurate interpretation of the speaker's message.

Below are specific strategies and techniques that can help build this skill effectively. Begin by choosing one or two techniques, and once you begin to naturally use them in conversation, add another technique (or two) to deepen your ability to empathize and communicate effectively.

Techniques for Active Listening

Reflective Listening

Reflective listening is a structured approach where the listener paraphrases and validates what was said before responding. For example, a teacher speaking to a frustrated student might say, "I hear that you felt left out when the group didn't include your idea. That must have been upsetting." This practice not only strengthens emotional attunement but also reduces misunderstandings by ensuring that the speaker feels seen and heard. To practice this skill, try repeating back what someone said in your own words, focusing on their feelings and the core message. The key to using this technique effectively is to paraphrase and avoid repeating verbatim what the speaker has communicated.

Mindful Presence

One of the foundational elements of active listening is being fully present. This means setting aside distractions, maintaining eye contact, and giving nonverbal cues such as nodding or leaning in. An effective way to practice mindful presence is through short mindfulness exercises, such as taking three deep breaths before engaging in a conversation, allowing your mind to focus directly on the speaker. It is also extremely helpful to put your phone away, remove any major distractions, sit in close but comfortable proximity to the person, and maintain an open posture throughout the conversation.

This kind of presence makes the speaker feel valued and opens the door to more authentic communication.

Open-Ended Questions

Develop the habit of asking questions that encourage deeper sharing. Instead of asking, "Did that upset you?" consider a more open-ended approach like, "Can you tell me more about how that made you feel?" Practice this by consciously replacing yes/no questions with questions that begin with "how," "what," or "can you explain."

Emotional Vocabulary

A broad emotional vocabulary allows you to more accurately identify and reflect the speaker's feelings. You can practice this skill by learning and using a diverse set of emotion words in daily conversations. Tools like emotion wheels (see figure 5.2 in Chapter 5) or lists of feeling words can help expand your ability to name emotions accurately.

Pausing and Silence

After someone speaks, pause for a few seconds before responding. This not only ensures you have fully processed what they said but also demonstrates respect for their thoughts. You can practice this by consciously counting to three in your mind before speaking.

Implementing Active Listening

Ms. Jenson

During a scheduled sensory break, Ms. Jenson noticed Malik, a third-grade student with an emotional-behavioral disorder, tightly gripping a fidget tool and kicking the wall in a steady rhythm.

Demonstrating *mindful presence*, she crouched to his level and said softly, "I can see you are upset about something. Want to tell me what's going on?" Her tone and body language conveyed openness without pressure, and her question was intentionally *open-ended* to give Malik room to express himself.

Malik shrugged, his breathing shallow and quick. After a long pause, he muttered, "They moved my desk again." Ms. Jenson allowed for *pausing and silence*, giving him time to process and speak in his own rhythm.

She nodded, maintaining steady eye contact. "I see, you felt settled where you were, and then they moved you to a different space without warning you. I get why that is upsetting." Her response modeled *reflective listening* and used *enhanced emotional vocabulary* to help Malik label his internal state with more nuance.

Malik's shoulders eased just slightly. "They don't care."

Ms. Jenson paused again before responding. She asked, "What would help you feel more settled again? Can you tell me what felt good about where you were sitting before?" She used a combination of *open-ended questions* and *intentional silence* to keep the conversation student-led.

Ms. Jenson's approach allowed Malik to explain that sitting at the front of the class helped him see the teacher and the whiteboard more clearly. Sitting in the back of the classroom left him feeling distracted and out of place.

Recognizing the legitimacy of his concern, Ms. Jenson walked with him to speak with the teacher. Together, they explained the issue and requested a return to his original seat near the front of the room.

Key Considerations: Ms. Jenson

In many classrooms, a moment like this might result in the staff member directing Malik to his seat, and when he refused or escalated his behavior, disciplinary measures would likely result. His behavior might be labeled as noncompliant when, in fact, it is a response to a legitimate concern that he was not able to immediately articulate.

When Ms. Jenson uses active listening, the outcome changes. By responding with mindful presence, reflective language, and open-ended questions, she creates space for trust and regulation. Malik is not only heard. He is emotionally mirrored and invited into a process that supports clarity and safety. His nervous system begins to settle, and he shows a willingness to reengage. What could have become another missed or misunderstood moment instead becomes a foundation for emotional growth and connection.

PERSPECTIVE-TAKING

Tool Number Two: Perspective-Taking

It is natural to interpret most situations through our own lens, but empathy grows when we intentionally set aside that perspective and view the experience from someone else's point of view.

Perspective-taking exercises build cognitive flexibility, allowing you to respond with greater understanding rather than assumption.[5] This skill not only enhances empathy but also fosters deeper connections and reduces conflicts in personal and professional interactions. Developing perspective-taking requires intentional practice and reflection, but the benefits are well worth the time and effort.

The techniques below are highly effective methods to cultivate this skill. As with active listening, begin by choosing one or two activities that you resonate with, then add additional exercises when you are ready.

Role Reversal

Role reversal involves imagining yourself in another person's situation, considering their feelings, experiences, and challenges. For example, a teacher struggling with a student's disruptive behavior might mentally shift perspectives, asking, "Based on what I know about this student, what is his behavior telling me? What does this situation look like through his eyes?" This practice encourages responses rooted in curiosity and understanding rather than frustration.

The same approach applies to an angry parent who storms into your classroom, questioning your teaching methods. Rather than becoming defensive, you might recognize that their anger likely stems from deep concern for their child's success and fear that their needs aren't being met.

Similarly, when dealing with an antagonistic colleague who criticizes your classroom management style as "too lenient," role reversal helps you consider that as a veteran educator trained in more traditional methods, your colleague genuinely believes structure and consequences are what students need most, and her concern is truly related to student success.

By regularly practicing role reversal, you learn to pause in tense moments to consider what underlying needs or emotions might be driving the other person's behavior, and you allow this understanding to shape your response.

Guided Reflection Prompts

Structured reflection helps shift thinking away from immediate emotional reactions and toward a broader, more compassionate perspective. Asking yourself prompts such as, "If I were in their position, what emotions might I be experiencing?" or "What external factors might influence their behavior?" can help build this skill. A practical way to practice is to set aside time after significant interactions to reflect on these questions, ideally through journaling or mental review.

Visualization Exercises

Visualization is a powerful technique for enhancing perspective-taking. Close your eyes and imagine the situation from the other person's point of view. Envision their surroundings, the stressors they might face, and how they might interpret the situation. Visualization helps create a mental representation of another's experience, promoting deeper empathy and cognitive flexibility.

Implementing Perspective-Taking Exercises

Ms. Rivera

Ms. Rivera, a special education administrator, was reviewing incident reports after lunch when she noticed that Jonas, a fifth-grade student with a history of trauma, had pushed over his chair again after being asked to clean up his space. The teacher had written that Jonas was "being defiant and refused to follow directions." Ms. Rivera felt her frustration rising. It was the third time that week Jonas had had an outburst.

Before responding to the report or addressing Jonas, she closed her laptop and paused for **guided reflection**. Drawing on **role reversal** practices, she asked herself, *"What might Jonas be experiencing internally when transitions happen? What does it feel like for him when he hears loud voices in the cafeteria?"*

As she considered his likely sensory and emotional triggers, something shifted. Instead of reacting from a place of frustration, she began planning how to adjust his transition routine. Her goal became one of clarity, not just compliance.

Later that day, she checked in with Jonas in private and said, "I wonder if cleanup time feels really overwhelming after lunch. It's pretty loud in there. Can you tell me what that part of the day feels like for you?" Her tone was calm, and her question was intentionally **open-ended**.

Jonas nodded and said, "It's too much. I feel like everything's moving fast, and I don't know what to do first."

For Ms. Rivera, what had been described earlier as defiance was now understood as a **stress response**. Drawing on the principle of ***role reversal***, Ms. Rivera adjusted his plan: Jonas would now receive a quiet signal and a written list of steps before cleanup time began. She would check in with Jonas to see if the new plan helped him to remain regulated and watch to see if the incident reports for Jonas decreased.

Key Considerations: Ms. Rivera

Behaviors like Jonas's can easily be interpreted through a lens of compliance. Without pausing to consider the student's internal experience, interventions often become reactive and misaligned. The result is that behavior continues, and the student becomes further misunderstood.

When Ms. Rivera uses perspective-taking, the dynamic changes. Her pause allows her to move out of immediate emotion and into cognitive empathy. She recognizes that behavior is communication and that emotional overload may underlie the actions she sees. This shift not only de-escalates future situations but also strengthens her relationship with Jonas, giving him the support he needs to succeed in a triggering environment.

NONVIOLENT COMMUNICATION (NVC)

Tool Number Three: Nonviolent Communication

Developed by psychologist Marshall Rosenberg, Nonviolent Communication (NVC)[6] is a communication framework that emphasizes understanding and expressing feelings and needs without judgment. It encourages empathetic listening and honest expression, promoting empathy in interpersonal interactions. NVC has been applied in various contexts, including organizational settings, education, and personal relationships, demonstrating its versatility and effectiveness in fostering empathetic communication.[7]

NVC is included here as a way to build productive relationships with peers, colleagues, families, and administrative staff members. Although you could technically practice NVC with students, it is best utilized to form meaningful connections and effective collaboration at the professional level.

Developing Nonviolent Communication skills involves practicing its four core components: observation, feelings, needs, and requests.

1. Observe Without Judgment

The first step in NVC is to observe a situation objectively without adding interpretations or evaluations. For example, instead of thinking, "He is being rude," reframe this to, "He interrupted me while I was speaking." Practicing this shift from judgmental thoughts to neutral observations can be done daily by noticing when judgment arises and consciously reframing it.

2. Identify and Express Feelings

NVC encourages expressing feelings clearly and authentically. This involves moving beyond vague expressions like "I feel bad" to more specific feelings, such as "I feel frustrated" or "I feel unheard." Building this skill can be supported by using an emotion wheel or keeping a feelings journal where you reflect on your emotions and practice naming them accurately.

3. Connect with Underlying Needs

Every feeling is connected to an unmet need. After identifying your feelings, explore what need might be driving them. For example, if you feel frustrated, the underlying need might be for respect or understanding. Practicing this step involves regularly asking yourself, "What do I need right now?" or "What need is behind this feeling?"

4. Make Clear and Compassionate Requests

The final step in NVC is expressing a specific, actionable request that can help meet your needs. Instead of saying, "You never listen to me," a clearer NVC request would be, "When I speak, could you please pause and listen until I'm finished?" Practicing this involves framing requests positively, focusing on what you need rather than what you want the other person to stop doing.

By integrating these four components into everyday interactions, whether personal or professional, you can transform communication patterns, reduce conflict, and foster relationships grounded in respect and compassion.

Integrating Nonviolent Communication

Ms. Kline

After a team debrief, Ms. Kline, a special education teacher, wanted to voice her concern about the new support schedule, which now assigns paraprofessionals on a rotating basis rather than keeping them in consistent classrooms.

Ms. Kline approaches her administrator using NVC and begins with an *observation without judgment:* "I noticed this week that our paraprofessionals rotated three times in four days. When they rotate that frequently, students with regulation challenges seem more anxious and have more behavioral incidents."

Mr. Dillard, the assistant principal, nods, but quickly adds, "We're just trying to be equitable. Every teacher has needs."

Ms. Kline replies by showing understanding, then *identifying and naming her feeling:* "I completely understand that, and I want to support a fair system. I am worried and a little overwhelmed when I see our students struggling with the different staff members moving through the classroom."

She clarifies the *underlying need:* "Students receiving specialized services need continuity, and many rely on strong relational anchors to have a successful day. I want to feel like we are setting them up for success."

She ends her conversation with a *clear request:* "Would it be possible to revisit the schedule to see if there's a way to offer more consistency without compromising the rotation system entirely?"

Mr. Dillard is quiet for a moment, then replies, "I don't want to derail students. I'm willing to look at the schedule again this afternoon."

Key Considerations: Ms. Kline

This exchange shows how Nonviolent Communication can move a conversation forward without conflict or defensiveness. Ms. Kline names what she observed, shares her feelings about it, identifies the need behind it, and makes a clear request. Each step builds clarity rather than tension.

By avoiding blame and centering the discussion on student needs, Ms. Kline shifts the dynamic. Mr. Dillard doesn't need to defend his decision because he is given space to reconsider it. The tone stays respectful, but the message is strong. NVC helps both parties stay connected to the purpose, which is setting students up for success.

TRAUMA-INFORMED EMPATHY

Tool Number Four: Trauma-Informed Empathy

While not yet a formalized clinical term, we refer to the following tool as trauma-informed empathy. The name reflects an emerging research-aligned approach that integrates emotional attunement with the core principles of trauma-informed practice.[8] Trauma-informed empathy is grounded in understanding that all behavior is communication. Challenging behaviors are recognized as survival or stress responses that students with a history of trauma develop to adapt to their environment.[9]

Research shows that when educators understand trauma's impact and respond empathetically rather than punitively, the results are improved student outcomes and reduced suspensions.[10] Studies also demonstrate that recognizing student behavior as part of a trauma response results in educators feeling greater empathy toward students and results in more effective interventions.[11]

The core principle involves a shift in thinking. Instead of wondering *what is wrong* with a person, you consider *what happened* to that person. This shift fundamentally changes how educators interpret and respond to student behavior.[12]

Like perspective-taking, trauma-informed empathy activates specific brain systems responsible for emotional regulation, meaning-making, and relational attunement. The themes and practices below outline a developmental path you can follow to strengthen this skill in day-to-day interactions.

Reframe the Behavior

Empathy begins with perception. When a student is dysregulated or disruptive, the default lens interprets their behavior as noncompliance. Trauma-informed empathy requires you to pause and reframe, asking What if this behavior is a protective response? What might this student be trying to communicate?

This reframing process reduces blame and activates curiosity, allowing space for a more accurate and compassionate response. It also begins shifting neural patterns that otherwise prime you for defensiveness. When educators interpret behavior as trauma-driven communication, empathy increases and interventions improve.[13]

Practice

▶ When a student withdraws, lashes out, or refuses, pause and ask yourself, "What is the student trying to communicate through his or her behavior?" Over time, this cognitive shift becomes more automatic.

Recognize the Survival Response

Fight, flight, and freeze are hardwired survival responses rooted in the autonomic nervous system. Trauma-affected students may remain in these states longer and be triggered more easily by routine stressors. Recognizing these patterns helps educators depersonalize the behavior and interpret it through a physiological lens.[14,15] Understanding these states reduces reactive discipline and supports co-regulation instead.

Practice

▶ Learn to recognize subtle indicators of stress and survival responses like clenched fists, darting eyes, or collapsed posture, so that you can engage in a way that de-escalates the behavior instead of escalating it. Many articles and books provide direct and subtle indicators of the fight, flight, or freeze responses, but the following website provides a free, downloadable booklet that lists trauma indicators for preschool, elementary, middle, and high school students. It is an excellent starting point to learn more: **National Child Traumatic Stress Network: Child Trauma Toolkit for Educators** https://www.nctsn.org/resources/child-trauma-toolkit-educators

Contextualize the Experience

Students with disabilities often face compounding sources of trauma. This can include medical interventions, sensory overwhelm, repeated social rejection, and academic failure. These experiences shape how they perceive safety and threat. Trauma-informed empathy involves holding this broader context in mind as you respond.[16]

By stepping into the student's lived experience, you deepen your emotional understanding and become less likely to rush to judgment.

Practice

▶ Before addressing behavior, reflect on possible contributing factors. Ask yourself, "What might this student carry into the room that I cannot see?" Consider the student's history by reading evaluations and IEPs thoroughly to have a better context for the student's behavior.

Focus on the Need, Not the Behavior

Responding to unmet needs, rather than reacting to the surface behavior, is a hallmark of trauma-informed practice. When educators prioritize safety, predictability, and connection, students begin to feel secure enough to self-regulate. Empathic intervention asks: What need is going unmet right now, and how can I help meet it?[17]

Practice

▶ Shift from "How do I stop this behavior?" to "What does this student need in this moment to feel safe and seen?"

Stay Regulated

Empathy is a relational skill, so your nervous system is a large part of the equation. Students will often mirror your energy, whether you are calm, afraid, or angry. Trauma-informed empathy can only be practiced when you are emotionally available.

Practice

▶ Review chapters on internal emotional intelligence development with an emphasis on self-awareness and self-regulation. If you are using these tools regularly or if you have mastered these skills, empathy serves as a natural extension of your own internal state.

Implementing Trauma-Informed Empathy

Ms. Raynor

During a mid-morning session, Ms. Raynor, an occupational therapist, is working with Leo, a second-grade student with mobility and balance challenges. They are practicing a seated core exercise using a stability cushion while Leo reaches for weighted rings placed to his left and right.

After missing the ring on his weaker side, Leo slumps back suddenly in the chair. His arms pull in tightly. His jaw clenches, eyes fixed on the floor. He stops moving altogether and states, "I'm not doing this. It's stupid."

Ms. Raynor pauses. She recognizes the signs immediately. Leo's frozen posture, clenched jaw, and a collapse in effort. This is more than frustration or defiance. Leo has a documented history of trauma stemming from early physical therapy experiences where repeated failure was met with pressure and stern correction instead of support. Those moments left an imprint, and even now, minor challenges can trigger that same nervous system response.

Rather than rushing in with encouragement, she gives the moment some space and engages in belly breathing to ensure she remains regulated. She says, "You have done a great job today, but I can see that your last try frustrated you. Do you feel like sharing what you are feeling right now?"

Leo shakes his head. Ms. Raynor gently pushes the weighted ring closer and says, "What if we changed the process today? Instead of reaching for the rings, we could stack them in your lap, or just pick up the rings and place them in a basket."

Leo's shifts slightly and says, "basket." As they continue, Ms. Raynor praises Leo for not giving up and completing the activity. Because she did not assume Leo was just frustrated or defiant, she gave his behavior context and got closer to understanding what he was trying to communicate. She stayed self-regulated, and empathy for Leo came easily.

Key Considerations: Ms. Raynor

What looks like defiance or disengagement can often be something far more complex. In Leo's case, a single missed movement was enough to trigger a classic freeze response. Without a trauma-informed lens, his behavior might have been labeled avoidance or oppositional. But Ms. Raynor's awareness of his early experiences with high-pressure physical therapy allows her to see the behavior for what it is: a protective response, rooted in past moments when his effort was met with harsh disapproval instead of support.

Ms. Raynor's decision to pause and regulate herself was essential. In that quiet moment, before offering reassurance or redirection, she ensures her nervous system is calm enough to co-regulate his.

Trauma-informed empathy means recognizing that behavior is communication. In this case, Leo's silence said more than words ever could. Mr. Raynor supported Leo's need to shift into another OT exercise, which made him feel understood and safe with her.

CHAPTER SUMMARY

Chapter 12 offered four tools and associated techniques that help you develop empathy, a crucial skill that paves the way towards productive communication. Research-based strategies to cultivate empathy support special education professionals in creating positive school cultures where both staff and students feel valued. Tools and techniques are summarized in Table 12.1 and include active listening, perspective-taking exercises, Nonviolent Communication (NVC), and Trauma-informed empathy.

TABLE 12.1 Empathy Tools and Techniques

TOOL	DESCRIPTION	TECHNIQUES
Active Listening	Fosters conversations that are focused on being present by reflecting the speaker's comments, acknowledging emotions, and asking qualifying questions to gain deeper understanding.	Active Listening Perspective-Taking Exercises Nonviolent Communication Compassion-Focused Therapy
Perspective-Taking Exercises	Encourages stepping outside of your personal viewpoint to consider another person's perspective. Perspective-taking exercises support responses that avoid assumptions and reduce conflict.	Role Reversal Guided Reflection Prompts Visualization Exercises
Nonviolent Communication	Promotes understanding and expressing feelings without judgment. NVC is successfully applied in various contexts, demonstrating its versatility and effectiveness in fostering empathetic communication.	NVC Components Observe Without Judgment Identify and Express Feelings Connect with Underlying Needs Clear and Compassionate Requests
Trauma-Informed Empathy	The practice of responding to others with compassion and emotional attunement, grounded in an understanding of how trauma shapes behavior, perception, and nervous system responses.	Reframe Behavior Recognize Survival Response Contextualize the Experience Focus on the Need Stay Regulated

Active listening encourages you to be fully present during communication, tuning into not only the speaker's words but also their emotional tone, body language, and unspoken meaning. This level of attentiveness fostered deeper trust and minimized miscommunication. Perspective moves you outside of your own assumptions, remaining open to the other person's experience, even when it challenges your expectations. Nonviolent Communication is rooted in empathy and honesty, helping you to listen without judgment and to respond in ways that strengthen mutual understanding. Trauma-Informed Empathy brings trauma-informed care practices and empathy together so that you can gain context and clarity on behavioral responses and choose an approach that can de-escalate behavior and meet your student's needs.

NOTES

1. Goleman, D., (2006). *Social intelligence: The new science of human relationships*. Bantam 2006); Roman Krznaric, R. (2014). *Empathy: Why it matters, and how to get it*. TarcherPerigee.; Wilson, E. J., III. (2015, September 21). Empathy is still lacking in the leaders who need it most. *Harvard Business Review*. https://hbr.org/2015/09/empathy-is-still-lacking-in-the-leaders-who-need-it-most; Nario-Redmond, M. (2020). *Ableism: The Causes and Consequences of Disability Prejudice*. Wiley-Blackwell.

2. Decety, J., & Lamm, C. (2006). Human empathy through the lens of social neuroscience. *Scientific World Journal, 6,* 1146–1163. https://doi.org/10.1100/tsw.2006.221

3. Singer, T., & Lamm, C. (2009). The social neuroscience of empathy. *Annals of the New York Academy of Sciences* 1156, 81–96. https://doi.org/10.1111/j.1749-6632.2009.04418.x

4. Weger Jr., H., Bell, G. C., Minei, E. M., & Robinson, M. C. (2014). The relative effectiveness of active listening in initial interactions. *International Journal of Listening, 28*(1), 13–31. https://doi.org/10.1080/10904018.2013.813234

5. Singer and Lamm, Social neuroscience of empathy, 85. Singer, T., & Lamm, C. (2009). The social neuroscience of empathy. *Annals of the New York Academy of Sciences* 1156, 85. https://doi.org/10.1111/j.1749-6632.2009.04418.x

6. Rosenberg, M. B. (2015). *Nonviolent communication: A language of life* (3rd ed.). PuddleDancer Press.

7. Rosenberg, M. B. (2015). *Nonviolent communication: A language of life* (3rd ed.). PuddleDancer Press.

8. Souers, K., & Hall, P. (2016). *Fostering resilient learners: Strategies for creating a trauma-sensitive classroom*. ASCD.; Jennings, P. A. (2018). *The trauma-sensitive classroom: Building resilience with compassionate teaching*. W. W. Norton.

9. Clinger, S. (2024, June 27). Negative behavior as a form of communication: How to be a trauma informed parent. *700 Children's Blog*, Nationwide Children's Hospital. https://www.nationwidechildrens.org/family-resources-education/700childrens?author=e9245179-c3c2-4d37-a7af-5d52f7c04129

10. Okonofua, J. A., Paunesku, D., & Walton, G. M. (2016). Brief intervention to encourage empathic discipline cuts suspension rates in half among adolescents. *Proceedings of the National Academy of Sciences of the United States of America, 113*(19), 5221 to 5226. https://doi.org/10.1073/pnas.1523698113

11. Koslouski, J. B. (2022). Developing empathy and support for students with the "most challenging behaviors": Mixed-methods outcomes of professional development in trauma-informed teaching practices. *Frontiers in Education, 7*, Article 1005887. https://doi.org/10.3389/feduc.2022.1005887

12. Substance Abuse and Mental Health Services Administration, U.S. Department of Health and Human Services. (2014). *SAMHSA's concept of trauma and guidance for a trauma-informed approach* (HHS Publication No. SMA14-4884). https://library.samhsa.gov/sites/default/files/sma14-4884.pdf

13. Koslouski, J. B. (2022). Developing empathy and support for students with the "most challenging behaviors": Mixed-methods outcomes of professional development in trauma-informed teaching practices. *Frontiers in Education, 7*, Article 1005887, 1–16. https://doi.org/10.3389/feduc.2022.1005887

14. Perry, B. D., & Szalavitz, M. (2006). *The boy who was raised as a dog: And other stories from a child psychiatrist's notebook*. Basic Books.

15. Craig, S. E. *Trauma-sensitive schools for the adolescent years: Promoting resiliency and healing, grades 6–12*. Teachers College Press.

16. Substance Abuse and Mental Health Services Administration, U.S. Department of Health and Human Services. (2014). *SAMHSA's concept of trauma and guidance for a trauma-informed approach* (HHS Publication No. SMA14-4884). https://library.samhsa.gov/sites/default/files/sma14-4884.pdf

17. Souers, K., & Hall, P. (2016). *Fostering resilient learners: Strategies for creating a trauma-sensitive classroom*. ASCD.

CHAPTER 13

Social Skills Tools

Have you ever observed a disagreement between two colleagues that quickly escalated into a heated argument? In such circumstances, the language between participants likely assigns blame, focusing on who is right and who is wrong, or perhaps an underlying lack of trust causes each person to assume the worst intentions of the other. Successful conflict resolution begins with creating meaningful, productive relationships through effective social skills. Maintaining a state of balance and composure throughout your interactions sets the stage for a positive outcome, so a degree of mastery in self-regulation skills (chapters 6 and 7) is required to effectively utilize social skills tools. Emotional regulation lays the foundation for internal stability, and social skills determine how effectively you communicate, collaborate, and resolve conflicts in a variety of settings.

Social skills are more than a series of behavioral techniques. When consistently practiced, these tools strengthen your brain's capacity for connection, adaptability, and leadership.[1] While empathy allows you to understand others' emotions, social skills determine how that understanding is applied in real-world interactions. By actively refining communication, conflict resolution, and relational strategies, you create environments where trust, motivation, and cooperation thrive.

We will provide four highly effective tools to develop social skills, outlined in Figure 13.1. Social skills, like all aspects of emotional intelligence, develop through practice. The more you engage, the more neural pathways supporting social cognition and interpersonal problem-solving develop. Over time, deliberate efforts to enhance social skills result in automatic, skillful responses under pressure. In high-stress environments, these abilities enable you to manage complex social situations, de-escalate conflicts, and foster collaboration with students, colleagues, and families.

FIGURE 13.1 Selected Tools for Social Skills Development

SELECTED TOOLS FOR SOCIAL SKILLS DEVELOPMENT

Conflict Resolution Strategies

Conflict resolution strategies provide structured methods for addressing disagreements in ways that preserve dignity, encourage problem-solving, and reinforce trust.

Structured Relationship-Building

This tool includes proactive strategies that foster meaningful connections. Techniques encourage trust, open communication, and a sense of belonging.

Social Awareness Development

Social awareness involves recognizing and understanding the emotions, needs, and concerns of others. Techniques increase sensitivity to social cues and improve the ability to respond appropriately.

Effective Communication Training

Structured communication training provides methods for enhancing speaking, listening, body language, and adapting communication styles to different contexts to enable clear expression and understanding.

CONFLICT RESOLUTION STRATEGIES

Tool Number One: Conflict Resolution Strategies

Conflict inevitably arises in professional and interpersonal relationships, but how you address that conflict determines whether the connection strengthens or weakens. These strategies provide structured methods for approaching disagreements in ways that preserve dignity, encourage problem-solving, and reinforce trust. They are particularly effective in building strong social skills, as they emphasize communication, collaboration, and empathy.[2]

Techniques for Conflict Resolution Strategies

Collaborative Problem-Solving

Collaborative problem-solving is one of the most effective conflict resolution strategies because it reframes conflict as an opportunity for mutual understanding. This method encourages all parties to share their perspectives, identify shared goals, and brainstorm solutions that benefit everyone involved. Rather than assigning blame, collaborative problem-solving focuses on creating win-win outcomes through open communication and cooperation.[3] To develop this skill, practice using "we" statements instead of "you" statements, such as "How can we find a solution that works for both of us?" Role-playing exercises can also help individuals rehearse this method in a safe environment.

Restorative Practices

Restorative practices focus on healing and repairing relationships after conflicts. These methods involve structured conversations where you encourage all parties to discuss the impact of their actions, express feelings, and collectively decide how to make amends.

This technique is effective in all situations, whether you are mediating student conflicts or addressing tension between staff members. In most cases, these conversations need a neutral third party to guide the process and keep the space safe for both voices. The following are the basic components of restorative practices:

- *Establish shared values*

  Begin by working with staff and students to define community values such as respect, responsibility, and empathy.

- *Introduce affective language*

  Model and encourage the use of "I" statements to express feelings and impacts, building emotional literacy and accountability.

- *Use restorative questions*

  In moments of conflict, ask: "What happened?", "Who was affected?", and "What needs to be done to make things right?"

- *Facilitate structured conversations*

  Implement regular restorative circles or conferences to address issues, repair harm, and strengthen relationships.

- *Respond to conflict restoratively*

  When harm occurs, prioritize repair over punishment by guiding those involved through reflection, ownership, and restitution.

- *Build ongoing capacity*

  Provide continuous training and support for staff to sustain a restorative mindset and embed practices into school culture.

Assertive Communication Techniques

Assertive communication strikes a balance between passivity and aggression, enabling individuals to express their thoughts and feelings clearly while respecting others. Using "I" statements, such as "I feel concerned when meetings start late because it disrupts my schedule," allows individuals to communicate their needs without sounding accusatory or defensive.[4] Developing this skill involves expressing needs and boundaries confidently while remaining open to others' perspectives.

For example, instead of saying, "That's fine, whatever you decide." You would say, "I'm feeling overwhelmed with last-minute changes. I really need more notice to support my students effectively."

Integrating Empathy in Conflict Resolution

In addition to these primary conflict resolution strategies, previously discussed empathy tools, such as active listening and perspective-taking exercises, also play crucial roles in conflict resolution. As noted previously, active listening requires giving full attention to the speaker, reflecting on what you hear, and validating their perspective. Perspective-taking enhances empathy by encouraging you to consider the emotions and motivations of others.

Emotional regulation techniques, covered in chapter 7, support conflict resolution by promoting a calm and thoughtful approach during challenging interactions. By integrating these approaches, you can navigate conflicts with empathy, maintain composure in difficult conversations, and strengthen your overall social skills.

Implementing Conflict Resolution Strategies
Ms. Nolan

Ms. Nolan, a middle school special education teacher, notices that Jordan, a student with executive functioning challenges, is refusing to give his peer a shared calculator during a small group activity. The peer is becoming agitated, saying, "He always keeps it." The two boys begin to argue.

Ms. Nolan steps between them and, using *collaborative problem-solving*, she says, "It looks like both of you need something for your activity. Let's figure out a way to solve this together."

She invites both students to sit at a side table. Once seated, she prompts each to explain how they feel about the situation. She guides the conversation toward shared needs and encourages them to work out a solution that feels fair in accordance with *restorative practices*.

After hearing both perspectives, Ms. Nolan models a calm tone and demonstrating *assertive communication* she shares, "I felt concerned when voices got loud, because I want this group to feel respectful and safe for everyone."

Jordan and his peer follow Ms. Nolan's lead and begin to express how they feel about the incident. When either student starts to blame the other, Ms. Nolan gently reminds them to use "I" statements to communicate what they need, not just what upsets them (*NVC*). Jordan explains that he feels anxious when he doesn't have the calculator, because he's afraid he'll forget what he was doing and have to start over if he has to wait.

Jordan's peer suggests that he's fine waiting, as long as Jordan passes the calculator over as soon as he finishes all of the steps to his math problem. Ms. Nolan asks whether this solution feels fair to both of them. They both nod. She offers one final suggestion: "How about we use a small timer for each turn, just to keep it balanced? That way, no one has to worry about waiting too long, and everyone knows when it's their turn." The students agree, and she hands them the classroom timer.

Before they return to their workstations, Ms. Nolan affirms their efforts: "You both did a great job staying with the conversation and working through it respectfully. That's how we keep this classroom safe and fair."

Key Considerations: Ms. Nolan

Disagreements during group activities are common, but for students with executive functioning challenges, these moments can quickly become overwhelming. Jordan's refusal to share the calculator was not just about the object. It was about his anxiety over potentially forgetting and having to start over, an issue he struggles with across subject areas. A punitive response may have addressed the behavior, but it would have left the underlying skill gaps untouched and the problem unsolved.

By approaching the situation with conflict resolution strategies, Ms. Nolan gives both students access to tools they can carry forward. Collaborative problem-solving shifts the focus from who is right to what each student needs to feel heard and included. Restorative practice creates space for reflection, allowing students to understand the interpersonal impact of their actions and to take responsibility without shame. Through assertive communication, Ms. Nolan models how to state concerns clearly and respectfully, reinforcing the idea that emotions are valid and boundaries matter.

STRUCTURED RELATIONSHIP-BUILDING

Tool Number Two: Structured Relationship-Building

Social skills extend far beyond conflict resolution. They also include pro-active strategies for fostering meaningful connections, which are crucial to creating highly effective teams and mitigating potential conflicts. Structured relationship-building tools create opportunities for deeper engagement and productive collaboration with students, families, and colleagues.

Developing relationship-building skills involves practicing specific tech-niques that encourage trust, open communication, and facilitate a sense of belonging. The following are three effective methods for building these skills.

Techniques for Structured Relationship-Building

Structured Team-Building Activities

Team-building activities provide a structured setting for individuals to engage in group problem-solving, cooperative games, or shared experiences that require teamwork. To develop this skill, practice participating in or facilitat-ing team-building exercises, focusing on active participation, listening, and support for others. Effective team-building promotes a sense of community and helps individuals learn more about the strengths and communication styles of others.[5] A quick online search for "team-building activities" will give you a wide range of options that offer a chance to step away from daily routines and learn more about the members of your team and community. Regardless of which activity you choose, there are things to include and what to avoid when arranging these sessions.

What to Include:

- Include clear objectives. Participants should fully understand the purpose of the activity.

- Ensure all activities are age-appropriate and sensitive to physical, emotional, and cognitive differences between peers.

- Always include time for a reflective exercise through guided questions, journaling, or group discussion, as this is where growth takes root.

What to Avoid:

- Avoid activities that may lead to embarrassment, exclusion, or vulnerability.

- Avoid overly competitive formats that may alienate some participants.

- Avoid overly complex instructions that may cause confusion or disengagement.

The same considerations apply when using structured team-building in educational settings. Using this tool with students creates intentional moments for collaboration, building trust, recognizing peer strengths, and practicing social-emotional skills in real time. Cooperative games, group problem-solving tasks, and reflective exercises allow peers to engage with one another in ways that foster empathy, communication, and a sense of shared responsibility. Whether engineering a joint solution to a challenge or working through a classroom goal together, students develop an understanding of how teamwork enhances outcomes and relationships.

Trust-Building Practices

As a special educator, you likely work with students who have experienced repeated social anxiety, failure, trauma, or negative associations with the school setting. As a result, many students with special needs are guarded, hesitant to engage, or quickly dysregulate in school and social settings. Trust-building, in this context, refers to your ability to create a reliable, emotionally safe relationship where students feel seen, protected, and respected. When that sense of safety is in place, students become more willing to try new behaviors, engage with peers, and tolerate social discomfort long enough to practice new skills.

Trust-building involves consistent and intentional actions that show reliability, honesty, and respect. There are many ways to approach this technique, but a few of the most basic practices offer a solid starting point.

- *Setting and maintaining boundaries*

  In a classroom where the rule is "Raise your hand to speak," one student often calls out without raising his hand. Instead of reacting with frustration or ignoring the behavior, the teacher uses the same calm response every time: *"Remember our rule—hand up first, then I'll call on you."* She applies this response consistently with every student, for every rule. Over time, students learn that the expectations are fair and predictable. This kind of consistency builds trust and a sense of safety (through predictability) in the classroom.

- *Following through on commitments*

  An assistant principal promises a student that she will come to her classroom before dismissal to see her drawing. Knowing how busy her day is likely to become, the administrator set a timer to honor that promise. The student develops trust that the administrator means what she says. This helps when the student struggles behaviorally, because when the assistant administrator comes to intervene, they start from a place of trust and confidence, making a positive outcome more likely.

- *Practicing transparent communication*

  When a preferred activity is canceled due to a schedule change, the teacher doesn't avoid the issue or sugarcoat it. She says, *"I know we were all looking forward to our art time. The schedule changed, and that's frustrating. We'll work on art tomorrow, and I'll remind you first thing."* By naming the disappointment and being clear about the plan, she builds trust through honesty. Students see her as someone who tells the truth and respects their feelings.

Each of these is a small moment, but in special education settings, those consistent, respectful actions lay the groundwork for meaningful relationships and social-emotional growth.

Although the examples provided relate directly to students, the same principles apply to colleagues and families. For example, when adults learn that you follow through on your commitments, set appropriate boundaries, and are transparent in your communication, they view you as trustworthy and are more likely to engage with you, even during tense moments.

Positive Reinforcement Techniques

Positive reinforcement strengthens relationships between colleagues and families by acknowledging and celebrating behaviors that support a positive school culture. This approach involves recognizing achievements, expressing gratitude, and offering constructive feedback. Practicing positive reinforcement can involve regularly highlighting what others are doing well, whether in casual conversations, formal feedback sessions, or written notes of appreciation. These practices help create an environment where individuals feel valued and motivated to maintain positive interactions.

The effect of specific praise cannot be overstated, especially when it comes to student interactions. As a special educator, you are likely familiar with the research from the Office of Special Education Programs' Positive Behavioral Interventions and Supports (PBIS) framework.[6] The PBIS model emphasizes that specific, behavior-focused praise strengthens desired behaviors and fosters a positive classroom climate by constructively reinforcing expectations. Sutherland, Wehby, and Copeland (2000) found that when teachers increased their use of behavior-specific praise, students with emotional and behavioral disorders showed increased on-task behavior.[7] When delivered consistently and intentionally, specific praise is a powerful and relationally grounded strategy for promoting behavioral growth and emotional safety in learning environments.

Implementing Structured Relationship-Building

Ms. Patel

Ms. Patel, a speech and language therapist, is considered an ambassador of school culture by her peers and district leaders. Each morning, Ms. Patel spends about fifteen minutes writing a short note to thank a staff member selected from two of the four schools she supports. Her gratitude is specific. For example, she expresses her thanks to a principal who created a private space for her to work in small groups with select students, explaining how his efforts contribute to accelerated student growth.

During her speech and language sessions, she reviews the rules and expectations with her student or group, and she follows through with calmly redirecting them each time a rule is not followed. Ms. Patel praises all students at a high rate (six positive reinforcements for every one correction). Her structure and consistency, coupled with positive praise, result in high student engagement and notable progress on speech and language goals.

Ms. Patel also makes sure to engage with families who make the effort to practice and support her interventions outside of school. She regularly calls or sends a note thanking them for their willingness to work as a team.

Recognizing that support specialists often are not attached to just one school, Ms. Patel volunteers each year to create and lead team-building activities for her peers and other related service providers, like occupational therapists and behavior specialists. These activities have resulted in an exceptionally strong related services team that shares ideas regularly and solves problems together. Even though she supports more than one school, Ms. Patel remains a consistent presence in each building. Staff members describe her as someone who listens fully, leads without ego, and builds bridges between departments that don't always collaborate. Her influence extends beyond the therapy room. She quietly sets a standard for professionalism, empathy, and shared responsibility that elevates the culture of all assigned schools.

Key Considerations: Ms. Patel

Building relationships requires intention. Ms. Patel's practices are an excellent example of how to incorporate this tool into all areas of work life. For students, she provides a predictable structure, consistent praise, and clear expectations, which creates a sense of safety and belonging. Through daily notes of appreciation, she strengthens staff relationships across campuses, and she engages families with gratitude and respect, recognizing their efforts to engage with the therapeutic process. Her leadership in team-building fosters a culture of collaboration that benefits both students and professionals.

Across settings, Ms. Patel models a way of working that centers active relationship building as a daily practice. Her intentional efforts shape both individual growth and the collective tone of the school communities she serves.

SOCIAL AWARENESS DEVELOPMENT

Tool Number Three: Social Awareness Development

Social awareness, which many people call "reading the room," involves recognizing and correctly labeling the emotions, needs, and concerns of others. This includes interpreting social cues accurately and adapting your approach to match social situations. Social awareness training provides structured methods for improving the ability to navigate social dynamics effectively.

This skill can be developed by practicing the specific techniques that follow. They are designed to increase your sensitivity to social cues and improve your ability to respond appropriately in various interactions, whether individually or in group settings.

Techniques for Social Awareness

Observational Exercises

Observational exercises place you in the role of "active observer." The goal is to focus on noticing body language, facial expressions, and group dynamics without immediate engagement. Reflecting on these observations helps build your ability to interpret social cues accurately and enhances your awareness of others' emotional states. The following are specific practices aligned with this technique.

- *Attention Discipline*

  Set a clear intention before entering any social space. Decide what you want to notice, such as tone, posture, or group energy. As the interaction unfolds, keep your focus on what is happening in real time rather than what you think about it. Quiet your internal commentary by redirecting your attention each time your thoughts drift or you begin to judge what you're seeing. Stay mentally present by avoiding multitasking and anchor your focus by watching carefully and listening fully. Use breathwork (chapter 5) or small physical cues like the feet-on-the-floor technique (chapter 5) to bring yourself back when your mind wanders. Afterward, take one minute to reflect on what you noticed. This daily practice strengthens your ability to observe clearly and respond with insight.

- *Active Social Scanning & Delayed Interpretation*

  Choose any setting where social interaction is naturally occurring. This could be a classroom, staff meeting, or therapy session. Silently observe the dynamics without intervening. Focus your attention on physical and nonverbal cues such as posture, eye contact, facial expressions, body orientation, and tone. Pay attention to how individuals initiate or respond to others—notice who dominates the conversation, who withdraws, and who appears engaged or disconnected. Keep your awareness broad rather than fixating on one person. The goal is to see the full picture of how people relate to one another within that environment.

It is very helpful to take notes during social scanning sessions so that you can review and reflect later, but use *delayed interpretation* to resist the urge to label behaviors or assume motives. Instead, record exactly what you see and hear. For example, instead of writing "He was frustrated," note "He crossed his arms, exhaled audibly, and looked away when asked to respond." Practice this technique with short, focused sessions. Only after observing multiple instances should you begin to interpret patterns. This approach helps build objectivity and reduces bias in social assessments.

Role-Playing Scenarios

Role-playing scenarios provide a structured way to practice responding to social cues and adapting to different social contexts. This technique involves simulating real-life social interactions, allowing you to experiment with various responses, followed by immediate feedback. Role-playing is particularly effective in building confidence and refining social skills in a safe and supportive environment. This practice is particularly beneficial for professional learning sessions or group learning for staff members.

There are many ways to incorporate role-playing, but the following are the top three methods used in professional settings. These techniques can blend easily into professional learning sessions or staff development activities:

- *Freeze and Reflect*

  Create a role-play scenario that mirrors a real social situation, such as a team disagreement or a conversation with a family member. As the scene unfolds, a facilitator or observer watches for a key moment when subtle social cues are present but easily overlooked, such as a shift in tone, body language, or engagement. At that moment, the facilitator calls "freeze." Ask the group or participants to describe exactly what they observe. What nonverbal cues were just displayed? What emotional state might be present? What assumptions might be forming? After the discussion, resume the role-play, allowing participants to use their new awareness to adjust their response. This practice helps slow down immediate interpretations and builds the habit of reading interactions more accurately in real time.

- *Silent Role Assignment*

  Create a role-play and privately assign one participant a subtle emotional role, such as anxious, withdrawn, defensive, or disengaged. Begin the scenario and allow it to unfold naturally while participants listen and watch. After a few minutes, stop the role-play and ask participants to describe what they noticed. Encourage them to reference body language, speech patterns, or tone of voice rather than general impressions. Then, reveal the assigned emotional state and discuss which cues were picked up correctly and which were missed. This exercise strengthens perceptual accuracy and helps participants practice identifying unspoken emotional signals.

- *Real-Life Scenario Rehearsal*

  This approach works very well in small groups. Invite group members to recall a real-life interaction that felt socially complex or emotionally unclear. Have them outline the setting, roles involved, and the specific moment that became challenging. Assign roles to others in the group to act out the situation as it originally happened, allowing the individual who experienced it to either observe or participate. Once the scene is played out, pause and reflect on cues that might have been missed, how the emotional tone felt, and what could have been done differently. Then replay the scene, this time integrating more attuned behaviors such as better listening, adjusted pacing, or clearer acknowledgment of emotional signals. This method brings personal relevance to the practice, helping participants build awareness and repair skills they can immediately apply in real interactions.

Develop Cultural Competence

Building cultural competence is an active process that involves expanding your exposure to diverse cultures, perspectives, and communication styles. Developing this competency not only strengthens social awareness but also enhances empathy and adaptability in interactions with individuals from all walks of life.[8] Activities like participating in diversity training, learning about different cultures through reading, art, and traveling, and cultural immersion experiences help to increase understanding and social nuances. The following are additional, specific techniques to build this important skill.

- *Guided Cultural Self-Reflection*

  Examine how your background, upbringing, and social environment have shaped your beliefs, communication style, and worldview. Begin with prompts such as: What values were emphasized in your household? What assumptions do you hold about time, respect, or authority? Who do you instinctively trust or distrust, and why? Write your reflections without editing or censoring. Then, review what you've written and identify where your cultural perspective might differ from others.

Repeat this process regularly to uncover blind spots and build the awareness necessary for genuine cultural understanding.

- *Engage in Cross-Cultural Dialogue with Reflection*

  Identify a willing colleague, peer, or community member from a different cultural background and invite them into a conversation about their lived experiences. Approach the dialogue with curiosity and openness, not to compare, debate, or validate your perspective, but to listen deeply. Ask thoughtful questions like, "What do you wish others understood about your experience?" or "How has your background shaped how you navigate certain spaces?" After the conversation, take time to reflect privately. What challenged your thinking? What assumptions did you bring into the exchange? What can you apply moving forward? This practice builds both empathy and flexibility in real-world interactions.

In addition to these primary strategies, previously discussed tools such as active listening, perspective-taking exercises, and emotional regulation techniques also support the development of social awareness. By integrating these approaches, individuals can improve their ability to "read the room," build stronger connections, and navigate social interactions with greater empathy and effectiveness.

Implementing Social Awareness

Ms. Ortega

Ms. Ortega enters the conference room. The family brought an attorney to the IEP meeting, and the environment feels adversarial. The father leads by stating that the district has failed to meet his child's needs, and immediate accountability is expected. As the Director of Special Education Compliance, Ms. Ortega noticed that the father's comments were directed toward her. Before speaking, she grounds herself, takes a breath, and silently uses *attention discipline* to observe without judgment. She acknowledges the parent nodding and agrees to consider accountability during the meeting

As the meeting moves forward, she tunes in to the group's emotional energy, focusing on posture, tone, and facial expressions. Each time the special education teacher shares information, the mother's hands tighten in her lap. When the principal speaks, the attorney stops writing and looks up sharply. Ms. Ortega uses

(Continued)

(Continued)

active social scanning throughout the meeting, resisting the urge to interpret these cues too quickly. The father's voice rises when the principal engages. The mother only speaks when directly addressed and seems to disengage when the special education teacher or principal responds. Meeting participants grow visibly uncomfortable when silence lingers.

Ms. Ortega writes down what she sees and hears and uses *delayed interpretation* to avoid drawing conclusions too quickly. She waits until the team pauses for input and quickly reviews her mental notes, considering what was observed rather than assumed. The mother's physical tension, the father's rising volume, and the attorney's shift in attention all point to moments that involved the teacher and principal.

Ms. Ortega said, "I can see that your trust in members of your child's team has been broken, and that is not what we want to happen. Let's start by slowing down a moment to clarify what has been said so far. We want to rebuild the trust we lost with you." The father sits back, and the mother's shoulders relax, giving Ms. Ortega the cue that she was correct in her interpretation. She was not assigning blame, but she was correctly reading the room and responding accordingly.

Though the meeting remained tense, the dynamic began to shift. The family shared specific concerns about a recent suspension and a perceived lack of communication from the teacher. Both professionals were unaware of these issues and immediately began offering explanations and solutions to the family's concerns. The tension dissipated, and the meeting progressed with greater collaboration and focus.

Key Considerations: Ms. Ortega

Social awareness requires presence, timing, and discipline. Ms. Ortega's actions show how this skill supports clear and effective leadership during moments of tension. Rather than reacting to tone or content, she remained grounded and fully engaged, observing the physical and emotional responses of everyone at the table. She noticed patterns that repeated, such as when the mother disengaged or the father's voice rose in response to specific speakers. She waited. She reviewed. And when she responded, it was with clarity rooted in observation, not assumption. Her restraint created space for the family to speak openly, and the conversation shifted.

Ms. Ortega models how social awareness can guide difficult conversations without defensiveness or urgency. Her practice of staying attuned to the emotional tone of a room supports more honest dialogue and strengthens the integrity of the process across every setting where it is applied.

EFFECTIVE COMMUNICATION
Tool Number Four: Effective Communication Training

Effective communication is at the core of strong social skills, enabling you to express yourself clearly, understand others accurately, and navigate complex social interactions with confidence. Communication involves both verbal and nonverbal elements, including speaking, listening, body language, and adapting communication styles to different contexts. Structured communication training provides practical methods for enhancing these skills, contributing to improved relationships and greater social effectiveness.

Developing effective communication skills involves practicing specific techniques that promote clear expression, active listening, and adaptability in interactions. The following are highly effective methods for building these skills.

Techniques for Effective Communication
Adapt Communication Style to Context

Effective communicators adjust their style based on the situation and audience. This might involve being more direct in a professional setting or more nurturing in personal interactions. To build this skill, practice observing and mirroring the communication styles of leaders or communicators you admire. Reflect on what makes their style effective and integrate similar strategies into your own interactions. The following are additional, specific ways to adapt your communication style to match the context of communication.

- **Audience Mapping**

  Before communicating, consider who's listening. Identify traits like age, background, context, and the dynamics of power and decision-making. Then ask: *What matters most to this audience? What kind of delivery will earn their attention?* Are you speaking to someone who values data or someone who responds to storytelling? Do they lean toward efficiency, or do they need warmth to build trust? Are you addressing a group with shared expectations or navigating a room with mixed roles and needs?

  Once you've answered those questions, adjust deliberately so that you can fully connect with the person or group, ensuring that they hear your message clearly.

- **Communication Style Inventories**

  Use tools to identify your dominant communication style and compare it to others to learn similarities and differences in ways to communicate. The Social Styles Model emphasizes interpersonal adaptability,[9] the

Communication Styles Assessment identifies four primary styles (analytical, intuitive, functional, and personal),[10] and the DISC Profile (Dominance, Influence, Steadiness, Conscientiousness) is applied broadly but most often in workplace settings.[11]

Once you have the results for your chosen questionnaire, identify your default tendencies, analyze mismatches, and practice adapting your responses. For example, an "Expressive" via the Social Styles Model may speak quickly, tell stories, and use hand gestures. A "Conscientious" communicator via the DISC may favor data and precision. By knowing your own style and analyzing the dominant style of the person or audience you are communicating with, you can adapt to ensure that your message is truly heard and understood. Remember, your message does not change, but how you deliver it might.

Communication Role-Play

Role-playing exercises provide a safe space to practice responding to different communication scenarios. These scenarios might include managing difficult conversations, delivering constructive feedback, or practicing assertive communication. Role-playing helps build confidence and adaptability by allowing individuals to rehearse and refine their responses in a controlled setting.

- **Scenario-Based Role-Play**

  This technique can be used as part of school, district, or group learning, or you can simply choose a friend or colleague to participate. Select specific interactions such as giving feedback, correcting misinformation, or responding to disagreement. Tell your partner or group members the role they will play and explain the context of the conversation. All parties should stay in character and allow the exchange to unfold in real time.

  Halfway through the scenario, switch roles to view the conversation from both (or multiple) perspectives. This is a powerful exercise that triggers empathy and a deeper understanding of the message.

  Once the scenario is successfully completed, debrief with your group or partner to analyze what factors affected clarity, tone, or outcome.

- **Script Rehearsals with Reflection**

  This is an independent exercise that focuses on high-stakes or uncomfortable phrases that come out differently than you intended. These statements typically sound good in your mind, but they seem to consistently create negative reactions based on the body language and the lack of receptivity from the listener. A few examples include, "I need your best work on this," or "I have feedback that will help you," or "We need to talk."

Select one or two of the phrases that seem to cause a negative reaction from others and begin practicing the statement(s) aloud, focusing on the tone and body language you use when communicating. Does your voice sound rushed, tense, or authoritative when you intend to sound supportive? Practice adjusting these elements while maintaining your core message.

Repeat the phrase multiple times, making small adjustments to your delivery. Focus on one element at a time: first your posture, then your tone, then your pacing rather than trying to change everything simultaneously.

- **Video and Review**

With permission from the listener, record segments of key conversations. Review the recording twice. First, observe posture and facial expressions without sound. Then watch again, focusing on pacing and vocal tone.

Look for patterns that either support or distract from your message. Note physical habits, vocal changes, or timing issues that affect how your communication is received.

Integrating Effective Communication
Ms. Garrett

Ms. Garrett, a behavior analyst, needs to present new intervention recommendations to two different audiences on the same day. Sarah's parents are data-driven and want evidence-based solutions. The school's treatment team includes relationship-focused staff members who prioritize Sarah's emotional well-being. Ms. Garrett opens the parent meeting by saying, "I have specific data showing Sarah's current intervention results and three evidence-based alternatives with measurable outcomes." She presents charts showing baseline data, current progress rates, and projected improvements with new strategies. Her tone is professional and direct, matching the parents' preference for facts and efficiency.

When she meets with the members of the treatment team later, Ms. Garrett adapts her approach entirely. She begins, "I want to share what I've learned about

(Continued)

(Continued)

Sarah as a learner and how we can help her feel more successful." Instead of leading with data, she describes Sarah's strengths and how the new strategies will build on her existing skills. She uses warmer language and "asks the team, How do you think Sarah would respond to this approach based on what you see in the classroom?"

During the treatment team meeting, the speech therapist pushes back, saying, "I don't think Sarah is ready for such structured interventions." Ms. Garrett's typical response would have been, "The data clearly shows this isn't working," but she knew that this phrase consistently created defensive reactions from team members. Through script rehearsals alone and with her supervisor, she had worked on how to deliver this message with a different tone and body language, and for this audience, that would be crucial. Paying attention to her tone and body language, she relaxed and used empathy when she stated, "I can understand why you said that. Sarah often pushes back when her schedule is too structured. But Sarah's data shows that what we are doing right now is not really helping her to grow. I am open to other suggestions if the team wants to share." The revised phrasing maintains the same message while inviting collaboration rather than triggering defensiveness.

Key Consideration: Ms. Garrett

Effective communication requires adapting your delivery method to match your audience's decision-making style and information processing preferences. Ms. Garrett's approach demonstrates how the same professional recommendations can be presented in fundamentally different ways depending on who needs to receive and act on the information. This makes all the difference in your listener or audience truly comprehending your information.

Ms. Garrett's script rehearsal practice enabled her to share the data—suggesting the present strategies were not working—with empathy and openness instead of in the authoritative tone that had consistently provoked defensive reactions. As a research-based analyst, she would not personally be offended by that remark, but she realized that other staff members were.

Ms. Garrett models how communication adaptation supports professional effectiveness without compromising the integrity of evidence-based recommendations.

CHAPTER SUMMARY

This chapter presented four research-based tools for developing social skills: conflict resolution strategies, structured relationship-building techniques, social awareness practices, and effective communication training, as summarized in Table 13.1. These tools work most effectively when paired with strong self-regulation skills, as managing your own emotional responses forms the foundation for successful social interactions.

TABLE 13.1 Social Skills Tools and Techniques

TOOL	DESCRIPTION	TECHNIQUES
Conflict Resolution Strategies	Provides structured methods to approach disagreements in ways that preserve dignity, reinforce trust, and encourage problem solving. Emphasizes communication, collaboration, and empathy.	Collaborative Problem Solving Restorative Practices Assertive Communication
Structures Relationship-Building	Promotes a sense of community within a structured setting outside of daily routines or within educational settings. Facilitates group problem-solving, cooperative games, or shared experiences that require teamwork.	Team-Building Activities Trust-Building Practices Positive Reinforcement
Social Awareness Development	Often called "reading the room," social awareness involves recognizing and correctly labeling the emotions, needs, and concerns of others. Includes interpreting social cues accurately and adapting to different social situations.	Observational Exercises Role Playing Scenarios Cultural Competence
Effective Communication	Forms the core of strong social skills, enabling one to express information clearly and understand others accurately. Includes both verbal and nonverbal elements including speaking, listening, body language, and adapting technique to different contexts.	Adapt Communication Style to Context Communication Role-Play

Conflict resolution strategies give you the means to address disagreements in a way that focuses on collaboration and accountability, lessening the possibility of power struggles or an escalation of the initial conflict. Structured relationship-building provided techniques that can be used with colleagues or in the classroom to strengthen relationships and foster meaningful collaboration based on trust. Social awareness development allows you to correctly

NOTES

1. Lieberman, M. D. (2013). *Social: Why our brains are wired to connect*. Crown.

2. Deutsch, M., Coleman, P. T., & Marcus, E. C. (eds). (2014). *The handbook of conflict resolution: Theory and practice* (3rd ed.). John Wiley & Sons.

3. Johnson, D. W., & Johnson, R. T. (2020). *Joining together: Group theory and group skills* (12th ed.). Routledge.

4. Alberti, R. E., & Emmons, M. L. (2017). *Your perfect right: Assertiveness and equality in your life and relationships* (10th ed.). New Harbinger Publications.

5. Klein, C., DiazGranados, D., Salas, E., Le, H., Burke, C. S., Lyons, R., & Goodwin, G. F. (2009). Does team building work? *Small Group Research*, 40(2), 181–222. https://doi.org/10.1177/1046496408328821

6. Office of Special Education Programs. (n. d.). *Positive behavioral interventions and supports. Technical Assistance Center on Positive Behavioral Interventions and Supports.* Retrieved January 15, 2025, from https://www.pbis.org.

7. Sutherland, K. S., Wehby, J. H., & Copeland, S. R. (2000). Effect of varying rates of behavior-specific praise on the on-task behavior of students with EBD. *Journal of Emotional and Behavioral Disorders, 8*(1), 2–8. doi:10.1177/106342660000800101

8. Sue, D. W. (2016). *Multicultural Social work practice: A competency-based approach to diversity and social justice* (2nd ed.). John Wiley & Sons.

9. Merrill, D. W., & Reid, R. H. (1981). *Personal styles and effective performance*. Chilton Book Company.

10. Murphy, M. (n.d.). Communication styles: A guide to understanding how people communicate. *Leadership IQ*. Retrieved January 15, 2025, from https://www.leadershipiq.com/blogs/leadershipiq/communication-styles

11. Marston, W. M. (1928). *Emotions of normal people*. Kegan Paul Trench Trubner & Co.

Closing Thoughts

At its core, this book is about empowering special educators. Its purpose is to help restore your energy and reignite your motivation so you can stay in the field, thrive in your work, and continue making a meaningful difference in the lives you touch each day.

Burnout is not a passing phase. It is a serious threat to the field and to those working within it. Yet little is being done to address the emotional toll this work demands. The tools in this guide are not quick fixes. They require consistency, giving the brain time and repetition to form new, supportive patterns. Over time, these patterns become the foundation for resilience, clarity, and long-term sustainability.

You may begin your emotional intelligence journey with just one or two tools. As your role evolves and your challenges shift, the tools you rely on will change too. This guide is designed to grow with you. It can be returned to again and again, offering strategies that meet your needs at any stage of your professional life.

If you are moving forward individually, look for simple moments where these tools integrate naturally into your daily rhythm. Notice when self-awareness diffuses conflict or when empathy transforms misunderstanding into connection. Transformation is rarely a single breakthrough. It is a continuous, lived process.

For school and district leaders, systemic implementation of these tools fosters a culture of emotional sustainability. When prioritized, they lead to research-backed outcomes such as increased staff retention, improved student outcomes, greater job satisfaction, productive collaboration, effective team-building, and more responsive leadership. For communities that seek a more structured approach, the author provides guidance, training, and consultation for integrating the tools in professional development initiatives.

The future of special education cannot depend solely on acquiring new skills. While technical growth remains essential, the emotional cost of this work continues to drive professionals out of the field. If the profession is to thrive, it must invest in the emotional capacity of its people. When emotional intelligence is embedded as core professional practice, educators are better equipped to remain composed under pressure, build authentic relationships, and lead with reflection rather than reaction. This shift will not eliminate the challenges, but it will create the conditions where excellence and endurance can coexist.

Index

Free professional learning from leading education experts

 **Live and on-demand webinars**

Get a certificate for PD hours!

 **Videos**

 **Podcasts**

 **Study guides**

 **New teacher toolkit**

 **Lessons and strategies**

 **Checklists and assessments**

 **Plain language summaries of education research**

 **Book excerpts**

 **Other downloadables**

 **Blogs**

Leave a review!
If you enjoyed this book, let us know by leaving a review on **GoodReads.com** or **Amazon.com**.

corwin.com/resources

CORWiN

CORWIN

To help every educator help every student

We believe   that every single student deserves a great education

We believe   that knowing our impact is both a privilege and a responsibility

We believe   that a fair, stable, and thriving society is built on education

ACO   363032